COURAGE IN THE SHADOWS

COURAGE IN THE SHADOWS

Understanding Anticipatory Grief and
Overcoming Its Emotional, Mental, Physical,
Relational, and Spiritual Challenges

CINDI DAWSON

Daylite Publishing

Copyright © 2024 Cindi Dawson

Dawson and Associates
Staunton, VA 24401

All rights reserved.

Printed in the United States of America

First Printing, 2024

Published by Daylite Publishing

All rights reserved. This book or any portion thereof may not be reproduced or used in any manner whatsoever without the express written permission of the publisher except for the use of brief quotations in a book review.

Paperback ISBN: 978-1-962270-00-7
Hardback ISBN: 978-1-962270-01-4

This book is lovingly dedicated to you, the reader.
May it encourage and enable you to meet
the challenges of Anticipatory Grief.

Contents

Introduction ix
Part 1 Emotional Challenges 15
    1 Shock 18
    2 Sadness 25
    3 Anger 33
    4 Anxiety and Worry 40
    5 Fear 47
Part 2 Mental Challenges 55
    6 Brain Fog 58
    7 Decision-Making Fatigue 65
    8 Problem Solving 72
    9 Lack of Motivation 79
    10 Loneliness 87
Part 3 Physical Challenges 95
    11 Insomnia 98
    12 Loss of Appetite 106
    13 Weakened Immune System 114
    14 Pain 122
    15 Fatigue 129
Part 4 Relational Challenges 137
    16 What to Say 140
    17 How to Help your Loved One 149

    18 Familial Anticipatory Grief 157

    19 The Unofficial Rules of Anticipatory Grief.................165

    20 Self-Care 174

Part 5 Spiritual Challenges 185

    21 Anger at God 188

    22 Feeling Abandoned by God.. 195

    23 Questioning God's Plan...202

    24 Inability to Trust God 209

    25 Spiritual Numbness 217

Conclusion... 227

Discovering Hope 231

Scriptural References All in One Place 234

Resources 253

Acknowledgements 262

Endnotes.. 265

About the Author... 277

Introduction

My phone rings about 2 p.m. with Mark's distinctive ringtone. Mark, my business partner / friend / brother in Christ and I talk at least once a day, often two or three times. He is not feeling himself lately, so he is undergoing some tests. I am expecting his call following his doctor's appointment earlier today, so I snatch up the phone as I return to my desk.

"Hey. What's the news?" I ask.

Silence. Then, finally in an uncharacteristically shy voice, he says, "I have tongue cancer — Stage 4."

No.

I can't hear.

I can't breathe.

I can't respond.

My stomach flips and the room becomes too bright. I can't feel my body.

My eyes burn from unwanted tears.

I crave something, but I don't know what that is. Chocolate? A walk? A hug? Maybe all of the above.

I feel like all the life has been sucked out of me.

I hold the phone, but I am suspended between reality and a soundless fog.

My mind flies into the future at the speed of light, seeing our business change, smelling the hospital room, and hearing the doctors' treatment options and recommendations. And I don't like a single second of what I am experiencing.

What will happen to Mark? How will he cope? What will happen to his wife and son? What will happen to the business? What will happen to me? How can I live through this?

It must take a solid minute before I can put myself together, breathe, and respond.

This is All About You

If you are holding this book, then you, too, have likely experienced something close to the previous scenario. What you experience and feel will change based on the relationship you have with your loved one. For example, Anticipatory Grief with a spouse will differ from what you experience with a friend from work or church. Every situation is different.

Right now, depending on your relationship, you are asking yourself questions like those above and many more, and you have absolutely no answers. You are probably afraid, angry, confused, exhausted, lonely, and even lost. You may also feel fragmented, abandoned, nauseated, and helpless. You may even be wondering why you are feeling like this when your loved one is the one facing a devastating future.

Know that your current state of panic is perfectly normal. You have received heartbreaking news, and you know that this difficulty is now part of your everyday life. When faced with a situation like this, everyone experiences countless odd sensations and emotions. All these sensations and more are the foundations of Anticipatory Grief.

But you are not alone. And while the situation may feel hopelessly endless, you do have control over how you respond to this experience and its effect on you and your life. It will not happen immediately, but it will happen. That is the purpose of this book — to share with you the reason you act and feel the way you do and demonstrate how to deal with these actions and feelings slowly and gently, reclaiming the real you that is missing right now.

When you understand why you are feeling and acting like you are, you will be able to recognize where you can make changes, implement them, and work your way back to yourself again. You will be able to focus on more than your grief and even look forward to having meaningful time with your loved one. You will be able to complete your everyday responsibilities, accomplish more on the job, and even speak with your loved one without feeling awkward. It may be hard to envision this now, but it will happen as you work through this book step by step.

Who am I?

Hi. I'm Cindi Dawson and before I say one more word, I want to convey my deepest sympathy to you for what you are losing and going through. As I write this, I am sending you a virtual hug and saying a prayer for peace in your heart. I will not demean you by saying I know how you feel because I don't. Every person's loss is unique. However, I will say I understand the struggles you are going through and will do my best to help you feel more like yourself again.

I'm a real person just like you who has experienced Anticipatory Grief four times. You already know about one of them — when my business partner, Mark, was diagnosed with Stage 4 tongue cancer. I lost one brother-in-law to several recurrences of cancer and another to amyotrophic lateral sclerosis (ALS), also known as Lou Gehrig's Disease. My mother was diagnosed with Vascular Dementia, and I watched her slowly fade away. I am even going through Anticipatory Grief right now due to my sister's uncertainty about the return of a rare nasal cancer with no possible treatments if it does recur.

While these challenges are not easy to endure or happy to look back on, they did provide me with insight into why I was suffering even though I was not the patient, and how to cope with and even change the symptoms I was struggling with. I have experienced and documented 20 of the 25 challenges in this book. I have compiled all my notes and suggestions I used for myself into this book to hopefully encourage and support you while you go through this same challenge. I also thoroughly researched and included facts and opinions from doctors, psychologists, and other experts about the topics discussed.

This book is organized into parts and chapters. The five main parts of this book address the Emotional, Mental, Physical, Relational, and Spiritual Aspects of what you are experiencing while each chapter addresses a symptom. Feel free to read the chapters that you need when you need them. I want this book to support and minister to you and hopefully give you the guidance you need.

Throughout the book I will use the term "loved one" to refer to the person you anticipate losing. This person might be a spouse, sibling, parent, child, close friend, work colleague, or fellow church member. But instead of a person, your loss could be a pet, location, or even financial support. Whenever you see the term "loved one," substitute who or what you are losing.

As you progress through your journey of Anticipatory Grief, you may face symptoms that you consider to be beyond your ability to manage. When that happens, feel free to seek help from a trained counselor, therapist, or pastor. You don't have to go through this alone. If you are at all experiencing distress, please consider asking for help from a professional. This person is equipped to help and walk beside you on this challenging path.

One More Very Important Closing Note

I am unapologetically a Christian, and this book is written specifically for those who have their hope in Jesus Christ. Trusting God to help me through difficult times is a natural part of my life. So, this book will contain scriptures, prayers, and suggestions pointing towards trusting God. But this book can also be helpful to those of you who are not Christians as it provides sound advice on managing your stress as you move through this challenging season.

The appendices at the back of the book include an alphabetical list of the symptoms covered in this book and the scripture references that apply to that chapter. If you feel that you need immediate support, feel free to jump to the Scripture References appendix, locate the symptoms you are facing right now, and read the scripture verses you will find there. You may locate them in your Bible if you choose, but they are fully included in the Scripture Reference appendix for your convenience.

You will also find a Resources section which includes names, websites, and descriptions for organizations and associations who can help with your specific area of loss. Feel free to contact them for more information about what to expect and ways to support and help your loved one.

If you are not a Christian or would like to know more about inviting Jesus into your life, skip to the Discovering Hope appendix where you will find a full explanation of what being a Christian is all about and how it can bring hope to your life, trusting God with your daily stress. Then return to the beginning and read the chapters that speak to you.

May God's peace and comfort bring solace and strength to your heart as you navigate the path of Anticipatory Grief,

Cindi

PART I
EMOTIONAL CHALLENGES

Anticipatory grief is a paradox between hope and despair, where your heart aches for a miracle, but your mind prepares for the inevitable. – Cindi Dawson

---

About six months after my youngest sister turned 13, I asked her what she thought it was like to be a teenager. She said, "I feel like I'm entering a long tunnel and it's DARK in here!" Although we laughed about it all the way through her teen years, I knew exactly what she was saying. She had embarked on a new journey with no flashlight, roadmap, signposts, or user's manual. And she was right. Seasons of your life can be dark and scary because you have no guidance. That's the way I felt each time I started through the Anticipatory Grief tunnel.

For me, the emotional part was most challenging. I'm normally a happy, optimistic person. My nickname in college was Sunshine. And as I grew older, I developed the mindset of, "If you're going to laugh about it later, you might as well laugh about it now." I still live by that tenet today. It carried me through difficult and embarrassing situations, and I enjoyed life more because I had this mindset.

But Anticipatory Grief was something new and emotionally I was a wreck. I could feel any number of distinct and separate emotions in the span of an hour. I would feel angry, and I had no idea why or at whom I was angry. When I was mentally lucid enough (We'll save that for another part in this book.), I would try to analyze the logic behind my emotions. And guess what? There was NO logic! I felt rudderless on a sea in a hurricane. I'm a "why" person, and if I can't identify why something is happening the way it is, I'm extremely confused.

When my sister turned 16, I checked in with her, asking her about life in the teen tunnel. This time she said, "My eyes are getting used to the dark." What a wise and insightful response to my query. She was letting me know that while her journey was still new and different, she was discovering ways to cope with it. I thought about that comment a lot while I was wandering through Anticipatory Grief.

It took months for me to realize that my emotions were not on a roller coaster. Roller coasters have quasi-predictable ups and downs. My emotions were on a trampoline with five other people, all jumping at the same time. If you've ever tried sharing a trampoline with others, you'll know what I mean. And the more people on the trampoline at a time, the harder it is to stay upright. That's exactly how I felt.

If your emotions are off the charts in an odd way, give yourself grace and know that you are perfectly normal. It may feel untrue while you're going through it, but I can assure you from multiple "up close and personal" Anticipatory Grief tunnels that it is normal. While you read through the following chapters, keep in mind that you can and most likely will experience these emotions individually and all at once. You will probably experience more than the ones addressed in this book. But the emotions included here are the most common.

My sister and I talked about her teen tunnel occasionally while she was "in there," and on her 19th birthday, I asked her if she finally had the hang of the teen tunnel journey. She said, "Yes, I feel better about it now because I can see the light at the end of the tunnel." Rest assured that I recognize what you are feeling, and my love and prayers are with you as you blindly make your way through the Anticipatory Grief tunnel.

I
Shock

Upon first getting the news about your loved one, you will most likely experience shock. While shock may pass quickly, it might take longer, depending on how close you are to your loved one and what your role will be during the Anticipatory Grief process.

Shock is the sensation that overwhelms you when you realize that something truly terrible has just occurred. This completely unforeseen event leaves you feeling immobilized and unsure of how to proceed. Unexpectedly bad news is usually the cause of shock, such as losing your job, a tornado hitting your area, or discovering that someone close to you — a dear loved one — has been diagnosed with a terminal illness. While other emotions may follow, shock is specifically a reaction to the unexpected nature of the event. This powerful feeling lasts only a brief time as it is so overwhelming that it would be difficult to sustain. However, it can recur without warning, more deeply tangling your emotions. It represents a sudden shift in your outlook, making you question your prior beliefs and wonder what else might be wrong.

Shock can make you feel disoriented, anxious, overwhelmed, and frightened. Knowing the symptoms and how to respond to shock is crucial to cope with the aftermath of a crisis and reduce the risk of long-term negative effects.

Symptoms of shock

During acute stress reactions, people can experience a range of physical and emotional symptoms due to shock. These symptoms may include:

Denial and disbelief You may find it difficult to accept the reality of your loved one's news and may not believe that it has occurred.

Anger and frustration You may become irritable, angry, and frustrated, directing your emotions towards others or yourself.

Repeated thoughts and memories You may continuously replay the event in your mind, making it hard to focus on anything else.

Emotional numbing You may feel emotionally numb, experiencing a sense of detachment from yourself and others.[1]

Rapid heartbeat and breathing You may experience an increase in heart rate and breathing due to the heightened state of stress.

Cold, clammy skin Shock can affect the body's temperature regulation, leading to a feeling of coldness and dampness in your skin.

Confusion and disorientation During a crisis, confusion and disorientation may occur as you struggle to process what has happened.[2]

The effects of shock

The most common side effects of emotional shock include:

Physical symptoms Emotional shock can trigger physical symptoms such as rapid heartbeat, shortness of breath, dizziness, headache, trembling, sweating, and loss of appetite.

Mental and emotional symptoms You may experience confusion, disorientation, difficulty concentrating, irritability, anxiety, fear, numbness, guilt, sadness, or emotional detachment. You may also have vivid or disturbing dreams, or intrusive thoughts related to the event.

Behavioral changes Emotional shock can lead to behavioral changes like restlessness, insomnia, increased or decreased appetite, withdrawal from activities or social interactions, avoidance of reminders of the event, or sudden mood swings.

Psychological impact You may suffer from post-traumatic stress disorder (PTSD) following emotional shock. PTSD can cause long-lasting symptoms such as persistent fear, distressing memories or nightmares, heightened arousal, and avoidance of triggers associated with receiving the news about your loved one.

Relationship difficulties Emotional shock can strain relationships, causing you to withdraw from loved ones, become distant, or struggle with expressing emotions. It may also lead to difficulties trusting or relying on others.

It's important to note that the severity and duration of these side effects can vary from person to person. Seeking support from a mental health professional can be beneficial for you coping with emotional shock and its aftermath.[3]

Ways to combat shock

If you are experiencing emotional shock, the top priority is to regain a sense of safety and comfort. Following is a list of strategies that may help you cope with emotional shock and restore a sense of balance

- Surround yourself with supportive individuals.
- Find a secure place where you can feel at ease.
- Enjoy your favorite snack or drink but avoid alcoholic beverages as they could aggravate your current situation.
- Take proper care of yourself or allow others to take care of you.
- Seek comfort from pets or comforting objects that are familiar to you.
- Engage in distracting activities, such as playing Tetris or video games, as they require concentration and can help manage your thoughts.
- Understand that you may not function normally at this moment since your mind and body are already overwhelmed.
- Avoid discussing or processing the situation while you're still feeling overwhelmed, as it could worsen the situation since your mind and body are signaling that it's too much to handle.
- Don't place excessive pressure on yourself.

- Ask someone you love and trust for a hug. A hug lasting at least 30 seconds can slow your heart and allow your mind to calm.
- Spend a few minutes in prayer or meditation.
- Listen to quiet, relaxing music.
- Respect your current state and allow safe environments, supportive people, and comforting objects to gradually ease you out of it without any undue pressure.[4]

While shock may be scary, it's important to understand that it is okay to not function normally during this time. Allowing time for healing and processing is crucial.

My Prayer for You

Dear Heavenly Father,

In this moment of heartfelt distress, I come before You with a heavy heart, seeking Your divine comfort and solace for my friend who is coping with Anticipatory Grief. I acknowledge the overwhelming emotions that accompany the sense of shock during this difficult time.

Lord, You know the depth of sorrow and pain that can engulf our souls when we anticipate the loss of a loved one. I ask You to grant Your divine presence to my friend who feels paralyzed by shock, unable to comprehend or accept the impending loss. Hug them up in Your loving arms, assuring them that You understand their pain and that they are not alone in their journey.

Father, I pray for the gift of strength and resilience in the face of this shock. Heavenly Comforter, gently guide their hearts and minds through the waves of emotions, allowing them to process their grief in a healthy and healing manner. Grant them moments of peace amidst the swirling sea of emotions, assuring them that You are the ultimate source of comfort and hope.

Lord Jesus, You too experienced the anguish of anticipation before Your ultimate sacrifice on the cross. I ask that You draw near to my friend, connecting with them in their pain and offering them Your perfect understanding. Help them to find solace in knowing that You have conquered death and that eternal life awaits those who place their trust in You.

Holy Spirit, be the gentle voice that whispers hope, peace, and reassurance into their hearts. Guide them as they navigate the complexities of grief, granting them the courage to face their emotions with honesty and vulnerability. In moments of overwhelming shock, provide them with Your divine wisdom and understanding.

Lord, I pray for a supportive community to surround my friend with love and compassion. May family, friends, and caregivers offer a safe space for them to express their emotions without judgment or pressure. Grant my friend the courage to lean on others, to share their burden, and to find strength in the fellowship of believers.

Lastly, dear Father, I pray that You continue to walk alongside my friend, extending Your unwavering love and grace. In the wake of shock, help them to find hope amid their pain, knowing that You hold their loved one in Your loving embrace. May the assurance of eternity with You bring comfort and peace to their weary soul.

I lift this prayer in the mighty name of Jesus, the conqueror of death and the healer of broken hearts, Amen.

Support from The Word

But You, LORD, are a shield around me, my glory, and the One who lifts up my head. Psalm 3:3

He gives strength to the weary and strengthens the powerless. Youths may faint and grow weary, and young men stumble and fall, but those who trust in the LORD will renew their strength; they will soar on wings like eagles; they will run and not grow weary; they will walk and not faint. Isaiah 40:29-31

Because of the LORD's faithful love, you do not perish, for His mercies never end. They are new every morning; great is Your faithfulness! Lamentations 3:22-23

The LORD is good, a stronghold in a day of distress; He cares for those who take refuge in Him. Nahum 1:7

"Peace I leave with you. My peace I give to you. I do not give to you as the world gives. Your heart must not be troubled or fearful." John 14:27

2
Sadness

Sadness is not the same as depression, even though the two terms are sometimes interchangeably mixed. It is an emotion characterized by feelings of loss, disappointment, a low mood, helplessness, hopelessness, lethargy, social withdrawal, crying, and distractedness. Sadness is a natural human emotion that can be triggered by a variety of events, such as discovering that a loved one is facing a terminal illness. It can range from mild to severe, and everyone experiences it differently. While it's a normal part of the human experience, it can be difficult to know how to cope with sadness and the accompanying negative feelings. In this chapter, we'll take a closer look at sadness — what it is and how it differs from depression — and provide some tips for coping with sad feelings.[5]

The Power of Sadness

Sadness is one of the foundational human emotions, alongside joy, fear, anger, disgust, and surprise. Despite not being seen as a positive emotion, sadness actually offers surprising benefits:

It gives strength in adversity. When you allow yourself to feel sad, it gives you the opportunity to rest and regain your strength. While sadness may make you feel tired and less receptive to the world, it is your body and mind's way of telling you to take a break and recharge.

It helps you confront your emotions. Sadness prompts you to look inward and identify the root causes of your pain, hurt, or anger. By recognizing what is bothering you, you can take the necessary steps towards healing and moving forward.

It allows you to seek help. Sadness is hard to conceal, and when you show your emotions, it sends a signal to others that you need support. It is crucial for your support system to be aware of your emotional state so that they can provide assistance when you require it.

It reflects on meaning. Sadness reminds you of the significance certain things hold in your lives. Whether it is a fight with a friend or a missed job opportunity, your sadness stems from caring deeply about your relationships or career aspirations. In this way, sadness helps you reconnect with your personal values, purpose, and passions.

It enables you to learn adaptability. Life is full of unavoidable hardships, and sadness serves as a valuable teacher. Through experiencing and overcoming sadness, you develop resilience and adaptability. What may currently make you sad can eventually become easier to handle as you learn and grow.

It forms connections. While sadness may leave you feeling vulnerable, sharing your sadness with others allows you to connect on a deeper level. By opening up and invoking empathy, you create bonds with others based on genuine understanding and support.[6]

The Effects of Sadness

Scientists have identified several effects of sadness on individuals. First, it enhances your memory by enabling you to notice and retain small details in your surroundings. Conversely, happiness tends to cause a blurred perception of time, as expressed in the saying "Time flies when we're having fun."

Additionally, sadness improves your judgment by diminishing the influence of cognitive biases, including how you perceive others. For example, you become less inclined to make snap judgments based on someone's appearance.

Sadness also serves as a motivation for change, reminding you that something is not right and urging you to make positive adjustments.

Furthermore, the vulnerability associated with sadness allows for greater empathy towards others, deepening your interactions and fostering meaningful connections.

Last but certainly not least, sadness cultivates kindness within you, as you are more inclined to extend help and support to others, hoping to receive the same in return.

How to Cope with Sadness

Acknowledge and label your feelings. It is important to be honest with yourself and others about how you are feeling. Don't suppress your sadness or pretend to be okay when you're not. By owning up to your emotions, you can better process and move forward from them. If it's difficult to share your sadness with someone else, start by acknowledging it to yourself. Look in the mirror and say, "I'm sad." You can also write down your feelings in a journal.

Allow yourself to feel sad. Don't punish or criticize yourself for experiencing sadness. It is a natural emotion that everyone goes through. Give yourself permission to feel sad without judging yourself. Find ways to release your sadness, whether it's crying, taking time alone, or seeking comfort from a loved one or pet. However, to avoid dwelling on sadness for too long, set a time limit. Allow yourself a specific period, like 1 or 2 days, to feel sad. Afterward, commit to engaging in activities that uplift your mood, such as listening to music, exercising, or spending time with friends.

Use creative outlets. Channel your sadness into creative outlets. Writing poetry, stories, or songs, and engaging in drawing or painting can help express and release your sadness in a positive and meaningful way. Create artwork that represents your emotions or listen to music that resonates with you. Sad music can surprisingly provide an emotional boost and aid in feeling better afterwards.

Recall past experiences. Remember times when you have overcome sadness in the past. Understand that sadness, like any other emotion, is temporary. Reflect on previous experiences and how you managed to feel better. This reflection can help you realize your capability to deal with sadness and remind you of effective coping strategies that you have used before, such as reaching out to a friend or seeking comfort from a pet.

Journal for clarity and progress. Keeping a journal can help you identify the causes of your sadness and make progress towards happiness. Write down your thoughts and emotions to understand the underlying reasons for your sadness. If your sadness is related to specific events or situations, write them down. This can help you brainstorm possible solutions to improve your circumstances. If your sadness is more internal, pay attention to your thoughts and beliefs. By writing them down, you can gain awareness and seek professional support if needed. Explore and capture as many thoughts as possible as they often reveal deeper insights.

Find reasons to laugh. People with a good sense of humor tend to be more resilient in challenging life situations, so try to seek out laughter. Spend time with a friend who always makes you laugh, or watch your favorite comedy movie or TV show. I have a Giggle Jar. It's an old plastic card file loaded with 3" x 5" index cards. I started it by remembering funny things that happened throughout my life, describing each one on a different card. Then when sadness struck, I would visit my Giggle Jar and read as many funny stories or moments as I needed to lift my spirits. Even if you don't use it to cheer yourself up, it's a great way to remember your favorite experiences.

Boost your positive emotions for an uplifting effect. Positive emotions have the power to expand your thinking and amplify themselves, offering solace during times of sadness. This is why it is crucial to actively pursue activities that generate positive emotions in order to alleviate your sadness. Fortunately, there are numerous methods to cultivate positive emotions, often easier than directly diminishing negative emotions. Enhancing positive thinking, practicing gratitude, engaging in enjoyable activities such as socializing, outdoor activities, or reading, are all ways to evoke happiness. Prioritize indulging in whatever brings you joy.

Sadness is a normal and natural human emotion that we all experience, especially following unexpectedly bad news. While it can be difficult to deal with, understanding what it is, how it affects you, and what your options are to combat it can help keep it under control.[7]

My Prayer for You

Dear Heavenly Father,
In the midst of the unknown and the pain of anticipated loss, I come before You with a heavy heart. I lift my friend to Your loving embrace, knowing that You are near to them, broken-hearted and crushed in spirit.

Lord, I see the sadness and grief that my friend carries within their soul. It is an ache that weighs them down, as they face the reality of an impending loss. I ask that You hug them up in Your comforting arms and fill them with Your peace that surpasses all understanding.

I pray, Lord, that in the depths of their sadness, You be their source of strength and hope. Help them to find solace in Your presence, knowing that You are intimately acquainted with their sorrow. Pour out Your healing balm upon their wounded heart, soothing the ache and wiping away the tears.

Lord, in their sadness, remind them of Your promises. Assure them that You will never leave nor forsake them, even in the darkest moments. May they find comfort in the truth that You are a God who collects every tear and holds them dear.

As they navigate the emotions of Anticipatory Grief, Lord, grant them resilience and the ability to take each step knowing that Your love surrounds them. Release the weight of sadness that threatens to engulf them and replace it with Your divine peace.

Father, I also ask that You provide my friend with a support system of compassionate and understanding individuals who can walk alongside them during this difficult journey. Surround them with friends, family, and loved ones who can offer a listening ear, a comforting presence, and prayers of intercession.

In the midst of sadness, Lord, help my friend to hold onto the hope that is found in You. Remind them of the eternal promises that await us beyond this earthly life. May they find solace in the assurance of reunion and the joy that comes from knowing You have prepared a place for us with You.

I pray all these things in the precious name of Jesus, who Himself carried the weight of grief and offers us comfort and hope, Amen.

Support from The Word

Even when I go through the darkest valley, I fear no danger, for You are with me; Your rod and Your staff—they comfort me. Psalm 23:4

Trust in the LORD with all your heart, and do not rely on your own understanding; think about Him in all your ways, and He will guide you on the right paths. Proverbs 3:5-6

Those who mourn are blessed, for they will be comforted. Matthew 5:4

For I consider that the sufferings of this present time are not worth comparing with the glory that is going to be revealed to us. Romans 8:18

Praise the God and Father of our Lord Jesus Christ, the Father of mercies and the God of all comfort. He comforts you in all your affliction, so that you may be able to comfort those who are in any kind of affliction, through the comfort you yourselves receive from God. 2 Corinthians 1:3-4

3
Anger

Anger is an intense feeling that can be caused by various circumstances, such as frustration, stress, or emotional trauma, or from feeling hurt. However, when anger takes over and becomes uncontrollable, it can lead to detrimental consequences. In this chapter, you will delve into the causes of anger, its effects, and some healthy ways to release rage.

Why do you get angry?

Anger is a secondary emotion. Typically, anger follows a primary emotion, such as fear, loss, or sadness. In the case of Anticipatory Grief, your sense of sadness and loss leads to anger because you want to lash out. Sadness and loss make you feel vulnerable and out of control, which can be uncomfortable. Sometimes, you unconsciously shift into anger as a way of coping with these feelings. Anger motivates you to take action to correct a situation and gives you the energy and strength necessary to do so.[8]

Anger can be triggered by internal or external factors. Internal factors may include stress, anxiety, fear, or depression. When these emotions become overwhelming, they can trigger anger as a coping mechanism. External factors that can cause anger include frustrating situations, injustice, or discrimination, or can result from feeling unheard, hurt, or betrayed.

One common cause of anger is a lack of control over a situation. Feeling powerless or vulnerable can lead to feelings of anger and frustration. For instance, if you are stuck in traffic and late for an important meeting, you may feel helpless and out of control. This can lead to feelings of anger and frustration.

Anger can also be a response to a perceived threat. When you feel threatened, your body's response may include the release of adrenaline and other stress hormones. These chemicals can trigger a fight-or-flight response and lead to feelings of anger.[9]

Anticipatory Grief can cause anger from several of these directions — stress, anxiety, feeling hurt, feeling out of control, or reacting to the perceived threat of losing the anticipated future with your loved one. With so many direct triggers, anger can easily become one of your biggest concerns.

Effects of long-term anger

Anger is a universal emotion felt across all cultures. When you become angry, you may undergo certain physiological changes. These changes include an increase in heart rate, elevated blood pressure, muscle tension, the release of adrenaline (resulting in a surge of energy), rapid or shallow breathing, digestive complications, and sleep disturbances.[10]

Although anger can have positive effects, such as aiding in problem recognition and providing the motivation to address issues, it also has its drawbacks. Research has linked anger to various health issues like heart disease, high blood pressure, sleep disorders, digestive problems, headaches, depression, and anxiety. Additionally, anger can prompt you to engage in risky behaviors like alcohol and substance abuse.[11]

Healthy ways to release anger

- Express yourself. Find a safe and constructive outlet for your anger, such as talking to a trusted friend or family member. Sharing your emotions can provide a sense of relief and help you gain perspective.
- Engage in physical activity. Channel your anger into exercise or some form of physical activity. Engaging in a workout or sports can release pent-up energy and promote a sense of calm.
- Practice deep breathing. Employ deep breathing techniques, inhaling slowly through your nose and exhaling through your mouth, to regulate your emotions and reduce anger levels.
- Use mindfulness and meditation. Incorporate mindfulness and meditation practices into your routine. These techniques can help you observe and accept your

anger without judgment, leading to increased self-awareness and control.
- Write it down. Journaling your feelings can be an effective way to process anger. Expressing your thoughts on paper can help you gain clarity and release negative emotions.
- Engage in creative outlets. Explore creative activities like painting, drawing, or playing a musical instrument. These outlets allow you to express and release anger in a constructive and enjoyable manner.
- Take a break. If possible, remove yourself from the situation that triggered your anger. Temporarily distancing yourself can help you cool down and gain a fresh perspective before addressing the issue.
- Seek professional help. If anger becomes a recurring issue that significantly impacts your well-being or relationships, consider reaching out to a mental health professional. This person can provide guidance and offer specialized techniques to manage anger effectively.
- Utilize relaxation techniques. Try relaxation techniques, such as progressive muscle relaxation or guided imagery, to release tension associated with anger.
- Practice forgiveness. Letting go of grudges and practicing forgiveness is crucial for your mental health. By forgiving others and yourself, you can free yourself from anger's burdens and find peace.

Remember, anger is an intense and natural emotion that we all experience at some point in life. However, when it becomes uncontrollable, it can lead to negative consequences. Identifying the causes of anger, recognizing its effects, and practicing healthy ways to release rage can help you manage this emotion more effectively.

My Prayer for You

Dear Heavenly Father,

I come before You on behalf of my dear friend, who is navigating the turbulent waters of Anticipatory Grief. As they grapple with the complex emotion of anger in the face of impending loss, I ask for Your divine guidance and comfort.

Lord, I acknowledge the anger that resides within my friend's heart. It is a powerful and overwhelming emotion that can cloud their thoughts and steal their peace. I pray that You meet them in the depths of their anger and help them navigate through it with Your wisdom and grace.

In the midst of their anger, Lord, I ask for Your supernatural peace to descend upon my friend. Calm the storm within them and replace their anger with a spirit of forgiveness, understanding, and acceptance. Help them to release any resentment or bitterness that may be holding them captive.

Lord, I know that anger can be a natural response to the pain and uncertainty of Anticipatory Grief. I ask that You give my friend the strength to express their anger in healthy and constructive ways. Guide them to find healthy outlets for their emotions, whether it is through prayer, journaling, seeking counseling, or engaging in activities that bring them peace.

Father, I pray for patience and compassion for my friend as they navigate the complexities of their anger. Help them to extend grace to themselves and others, understanding that anger is a normal and valid emotion in their grief journey.

May the power of Your Holy Spirit, Lord, help my friend to gain perspective and empathy in their anger. Teach them to see through Your eyes, recognizing the hurt and pain that others may be experiencing. Empower them to offer forgiveness and grace, even during their own struggles.

Lord, I ask that You surround my friend with a community of understanding and supportive individuals who can provide a listening ear, wise counsel, and love. Help them find spaces where their anger can be acknowledged, embraced, and transformed in the light of Your love.

Above all, Lord, I pray that my friend finds solace in Your presence. Remind them that You are a God who understands their anger and walks with them through every stage of grief. Fill them with Your peace, which surpasses all understanding, and heal the deep wounds that anger has caused.

In the name of Jesus, who can empathize with anger and offers us restoration and peace, I pray, Amen.

Support from The Word

The LORD is the One who will go before you. He will be with you; He will not leave you or forsake you. Do not be afraid or discouraged. Deuteronomy 31:8

Refrain from anger and give up your rage; do not be agitated—it can only bring harm. For evildoers will be destroyed, but those who put their hope in the LORD will inherit the land. Psalm 37:8-9

May the LORD, Maker of heaven and earth, bless you from Zion. Psalm 134:3

A fool gives full vent to his anger, but a wise man holds it in check. Proverbs 29:11

My dearly loved brothers, understand this. Everyone must be quick to hear, slow to speak, and slow to anger, for man's anger does not accomplish God's righteousness. James 1:19-20

4
ANXIETY AND WORRY

According to Dictionary.com, the definition of worry is "to torment oneself with or suffer from disturbing thoughts."[12] You may have another definition, but no matter how you define it, worrying is frustrating, intrusive, and stressful. You might worry about your loved one's decline or your future without them, and even how you will adapt as you pass through the Anticipatory Grief journey.

In this chapter you will discover the differences between worry and anxiety, what the symptoms of anxiety are, and how you can reduce worry and anxiety. Knowing and understanding can help you navigate each day and avoid more complicated effects of both worry and anxiety.

Difference between worry and anxiety

Worry and anxiety are words often used interchangeably, but there are distinct differences between the two. Worry is typically temporary, arising from concerns or uncertainties about specific situations. It can prompt problem-solving and decision-making, leading to action and resolution. While worry may cause some discomfort, it usually does not significantly impair daily functioning.

On the other hand, anxiety is a more persistent and pervasive state of unease or fear. It often arises without a specific trigger or can be disproportionate to the situation at hand. Anxiety can feel overwhelming and may interfere with daily activities, relationships, and overall well-being.

Understanding the differences between worry and anxiety is crucial when it comes to managing and seeking appropriate support. Recognizing worry as a fleeting response to a specific problem can help you engage in problem-solving techniques to tackle the issue. In contrast, acknowledging anxiety as a more chronic condition can prompt the need for professional intervention, therapy, or other treatment approaches.[13]

Overall, worry is a temporary response that motivates you to address specific concerns, while anxiety is a more enduring state that can significantly impact one's ability to function. Being aware of these distinctions can aid in recognizing and addressing these emotional experiences effectively.

Are you suffering from anxiety?

How can you tell if you are experiencing anxiety? Answer the following questions to get a better view of your situation.

Do you ever find yourself getting annoyed with people or situations, without really knowing why? Perhaps you start tapping your fingers impatiently when church runs 10 minutes late, or you withdraw from group situations after an awkward moment. This excessive agitation you experience is a sign of anxiety.

Feeling tired and fatigued all the time? Anxiety disorders directly impact sleep, and you might not even realize how serious the effect is. It may be worth mentioning this symptom to your doctor, as anxiety could be the cause of your constantly sleepy eyes.

Having trouble focusing or experiencing fuzzy thoughts? If you find yourself squinting at your computer screen for extended periods or struggling to come up with simple words, anxiety might be the culprit. Brain fog and related symptoms, such as difficulty focusing or short-term memory problems, are common signs of anxiety.

Feeling tense and experiencing muscle soreness? Anxious individuals tend to unconsciously clench their muscles, leading to a sore jaw, tensed temples, and achy legs. This is nothing to panic about — it's just another symptom of anxiety.

It's no surprise that panic attacks are a sign of anxiety, but do you always recognize when you're having one? Pay attention to your body's reactions and your emotions during these frightening episodes or when your heart is racing. It may not be just a physiological response — it could be a panic attack.

Do you frequently cancel plans at the last minute? Are you known among your friends as "the person who never shows up"? Avoiding social situations that cause stress is a quite common symptom of anxiety.[14]

Ways to reduce worry and anxiety

Practice relaxation techniques such as deep breathing, progressive muscle relaxation, or yoga.
    Set aside a specific time each day to worry as much as you want, but when the time is up, stop.
    Redirect your thoughts to the present.
    Exercise regularly.
    Talk to friends, family, or a mental health provider.
    Identify the triggers that make you worry or become anxious.
    Write down what is worrying you or making you anxious, getting it out of your head.
    Relax and practice mindfulness.[15]

    Anxiety and worry are common, but this does not mean that they need to control your thoughts and actions. By implementing some of these strategies, you can learn to manage and eventually overcome these feelings. Seeking help from a mental health professional can also assist in identifying the root causes and improving overall well-being. Remember, it is possible to live a life free of anxiety and worry, and it starts with taking steps to create change.

My Prayer for You

Dear Heavenly Father,
    I come before You with a heavy heart, lifting my friend to Your loving care as they face the weight of Anticipatory Grief. I seek Your divine intervention and comfort for the

overwhelming emotions of worry and anxiety that consume their being.

Lord, I recognize the burdensome worry and anxiety that my friend carries within their soul. The fear of the unknown, the anticipation of loss, and the constant thoughts of what lies ahead weigh heavily on their heart and mind. I ask that You gently calm their troubled spirit and replace their worries with Your perfect peace.

In the midst of their worry and anxiety, give them the strength to surrender their fears into Your capable hands. Help them to trust in Your sovereign plan, knowing that You hold every moment of their life in Your loving embrace. Grant them the assurance that You are orchestrating every detail for their ultimate good.

Father, I pray that You grant my friend the ability to release the burdens of worry and anxiety that threaten to overwhelm them. Surround them with Your divine presence, filling their heart with a deep sense of peace that can only come from You.

Guard their thoughts, Lord, and shield them from crippling anxiety. Replace their worries with a steadfast faith in Your faithfulness and provision. Remind them that You are their ever-present help in times of trouble and that nothing is too difficult for You.

Father, I ask that You provide my friend with the strength and courage to surrender their worries to You in prayer. Give them the confidence to pour out their anxieties at Your feet, knowing that You are listening and ready to offer comfort and guidance.

In the midst of their worry and anxiety, Lord, surround them with a supportive community. Place understanding friends, family members, and counselors in their path who can provide a listening ear, words of encouragement, and prayers of intercession.

Above all, Lord, I pray that You strengthen my friend's faith and give them the assurance that You are with them every step of the way. Help them to anchor their hope in You, knowing that You are the source of true peace and the one who can ease their troubled mind.

In the name of Jesus, who offers rest to the weary and peace to the anxious, I pray, Amen.

Support from The Word

The Lord is a refuge for the oppressed, a refuge in times of trouble. Psalm 9:9

Anxiety in a man's heart weighs it down, but a good word cheers it up. Proverbs 12:25

This is why I tell you; Don't worry about your life, what you will eat or what you will drink; or about your body, what you will wear. Isn't life more than food and the body more than clothing? Look at the birds of the sky. They don't sow or reap or gather into barns, yet your heavenly Father feeds them. Aren't you worth more than they? Can any of you add a single cubit to his height by worrying? And why do you worry about clothes? Learn how the wildflowers of the field grow; they don't labor or spin thread. Yet I tell you that not even Solomon in all his splendor was adorned like one of these! If that's how God clothes the grass of the field, which is here today and thrown into the furnace tomorrow, won't He do much more for you— you of little faith? So don't worry, saying, "What will you eat?" or "What will you drink?" or "What will you wear?" For the idolaters eagerly seek all these things, and your heavenly Father knows that you need them. But seek first the kingdom of God and His righteousness, and all these things will be provided for you. Therefore, don't worry about tomorrow because tomorrow will worry about itself. Each day has enough trouble of its own. Matthew 6:25-34

We know that all things work together for the good of those who love God; those who are called according to His purpose. Romans 8:28

Don't worry about anything, but in everything, through prayer and petition with thanksgiving, let your requests be made known to God. And the peace of God, which surpasses every thought, will guard your hearts and minds in Christ Jesus. Philippians 4:6-7

5
Fear

Fear is an emotion that everyone experiences at some point in their life. It's a completely normal response to danger or perceived threats. However, when fear takes hold of you, it can be debilitating and can keep you from living your life to the fullest.

What Is fear?

Fear is a natural human emotion that has evolutionary roots. It is a response to perceived danger or threat that triggers the fight-or-flight response in the body. For your ancestors, this response helped them survive in the face of real physical dangers. In modern times, the cause of fear has evolved to include social and situational threats, such as public speaking, job interviews, or the impending loss of a loved one.

The amygdala, a structure in the brain, plays a key role in fear. When it senses a threat, it sends signals to the hypothalamus, which activates the sympathetic nervous system. The sympathetic nervous system then releases adrenaline and other stress hormones that prepare the body for fight or flight. This response can be helpful in an actual dangerous situation, but when the perceived threat is not physically real, it can lead to unnecessary anxiety and panic.[16]

Symptoms of fear

Physical symptoms can manifest in individuals experiencing fear. You might encounter the following physical symptoms: sensations of being unsteady, dizzy, lightheaded, or faint; or a feeling of choking. These symptoms could also present as a pounding heart, palpitations, or a faster heart rate; chest pain or a sensation of tightness in the chest; sweating; hot or cold flushes; shortness of breath or a feeling of smothering. These symptoms may even be experienced as nausea, vomiting, or diarrhea; numbness or tingling sensations; or trembling or shaking.[17]

Effects of chronic fear

The impact of chronic fear is significant. It has detrimental effects on both our physical and mental health.

Physically, fear weakens our immune system, making us more susceptible to illness. It can also lead to cardiovascular damage, ulcers, irritable bowel syndrome, and decreased fertility. Moreover, chronic fear can accelerate the aging process and even contribute to premature death.

Mentally, fear can impair our ability to form long-term memories and damage specific areas of the brain, such as the hippocampus which affects our learning, memory, and reactions. This can result in difficulty regulating fear and constant anxiety. To someone experiencing chronic fear, the world appears frightening, further reinforcing their fearful memories.

Furthermore, fear disrupts brain processes that allow us to regulate emotions, interpret non-verbal cues, think before acting, and make ethical decisions. These disruptions negatively impact our thinking and decision-making abilities, leaving us vulnerable to intense emotions and impulsive reactions. Consequently, chronic fear can render us incapable of acting appropriately.

Lastly, long-term fear can also lead to fatigue, clinical depression, and post-traumatic stress disorder (PTSD), further exacerbating the mental health consequences of living in a state of constant fear.[18]

Overcoming fear

While fear can be debilitating, there are many ways to manage and overcome it. Here are ten mental hacks to help conquer fear:

- Let go of control. You may try to control every aspect of your lives to ward off fear and anxiety. However, sometimes it's important to recognize what is outside of your control and let go of the outcome.

- Change your self-talk. The way you talk to yourself can have an enormous impact on your emotions. Replace negative self-talk with supportive, encouraging words.
- Practice mindfulness. Mindfulness techniques, such as meditation or deep breathing, can help you stay present and grounded in the face of fear. This can help you avoid getting caught up in worst-case scenarios.
- Find a support system. Surround yourself with supportive people who can help you navigate fearful situations and who can provide you with encouragement and guidance.
- Reframe the situation. Instead of focusing on what could go wrong, try to reframe the situation in a more positive light. For example, if you're anxious about a job interview, focus on the opportunity to learn more about the company and meet new people.
- Face your fear. Avoidance can actually make fear worse. Try to gradually confront your fear in small steps to desensitize yourself to it.
- Challenge your assumptions. Fear is often fueled by assumptions and beliefs that may not be accurate. Try to challenge these assumptions with rational and logical thinking.
- Use your imagination. Visualization techniques can be a powerful tool for managing fear. Imagine yourself succeeding in a fearful situation, and focus on the feeling of success and accomplishment.
- Learn relaxation techniques. Incorporate relaxation techniques, such as deep breathing exercises or meditation, to calm your mind and body when facing your fears. These techniques can help reduce anxiety

and allow you to approach challenging situations more calmly.
- Celebrate your successes. Acknowledge and reward yourself for each step you take towards overcoming your fears. Recognize that progress may be gradual and self-compassion is essential throughout the journey. Celebrating your triumphs will motivate you to continue pushing forward.[19]

While fear can be a natural and normal response to Anticipatory Grief, it can also be debilitating and hold you back from fully living your life. By understanding the psychology of fear and taking steps to manage and overcome it, you can learn to move past your fear and live more fully. Whether it's practicing mindfulness, finding a support system, or challenging your assumptions, there are many ways to conquer fear and lead a more fulfilling life.

My Prayer for You

Dear Heavenly Father,
 I come before You with a heart burdened for my dear friend, who is grappling with the overwhelming emotion of fear in the face of Anticipatory Grief. I lift my friend to Your loving arms, seeking Your divine comfort and peace in the midst of their fears.
 Lord, I see the fear that grips my friend's heart and causes anxiety to consume their thoughts. It is a paralyzing emotion that robs them of joy, peace, and the ability to fully trust in Your unfailing love and faithfulness. I ask that You meet them in their fear and guide them towards a place of courage and trust in You.

In the midst of their fear, Lord, I pray that You be their refuge and stronghold. Help them to find peace in the truth of Your Word, which assures us that we need not be afraid, for You are with us. Remind my friend of Your constancy, love, and unwavering presence, even in the midst of their darkest fears.

Father, I ask that You calm the anxious thoughts and racing heartbeat of my dear friend. Replace their fears with a deep sense of trust in Your perfect plan and sovereign care. When worry overwhelms them, help them to fix their eyes on You, knowing that You hold their life and their loved one's life in Your hands.

Lord, I pray that You grant my friend strength and courage to face their fears head-on. Empower them to confront their anxieties with faith and hope, knowing that You are in control. Grant them the ability to surrender their fears to You, finding refuge and security in the shadow of Your wings.

In the face of fear, Lord, provide my friend with a community of devoted believers who can offer support, encouragement, and prayers. Surround them with compassionate individuals who can walk alongside them in this season of Anticipatory Grief.

Above all, Lord, I ask that You strengthen my dear friend's faith and help them cling to Your promises. Grant them peace that defies understanding and guards their heart and mind. May their faith in Your steadfast love overshadow the grip of fear, enabling them to live with courage and hope.

In the name of Jesus, who conquered fear and offers us peace, I pray, Amen.

Support from The Word

The LORD is the One who will go before you. He will be with you; He will not leave you or forsake you. Do not be afraid or discouraged. Deuteronomy 31:8

The LORD is my light and my salvation—whom should I fear? The LORD is the stronghold of my life—of whom should I be afraid? When evildoers came against me to devour my flesh, my foes and my enemies stumbled and fell. Though an army deploys against me, my heart is not afraid; though a war breaks out against me, still I am confident. Psalm 27:1-3

When I am afraid, I will trust in You. In God, whose word I praise, in God I trust; I will not fear. What can man do to me? Psalm 56:3-4

Indeed, the hairs of your head are all counted. Don't be afraid; you are worth more than many sparrows! Luke 12:7

Now you have this treasure in clay jars, so that this extraordinary power may be from God and not from us. You are pressured in every way but not crushed; you are perplexed but not in despair; you are persecuted but not abandoned; you are struck down but not destroyed. 2 Corinthians 4:7-9

Part 2
Mental Challenges

> Anticipatory grief is an unending storm that robs your mind of clarity, making even the simplest tasks feel like an uphill battle.
> – Cindi Dawson

It happened at the corner of Nutley and Tapawingo. My younger sister was driving with a learner's permit. With Daddy's permission, she settled behind the wheel, my parents joining her in the front seat while my other two sisters and I took our appointed places in the back for a typical trip home from church. What the five of us didn't know was that my sister had not quite mastered the art of turning. We approached the intersection - with no light or stop sign, and she turned right going 35 mph. Suddenly, the back seat occupants slammed into the left-hand door, smashing my youngest sister in the process. (Sorry about that, Sweetie.) All six of us - plus the car, were fine, but it was an eye-opening experience.

Anticipatory Grief can be as surprising as turning a corner at 35 mph, but as unbelievable as it seems, you can learn a lot with every new challenge you face. You can share your challenges and successes with your future self and learn from them both now and later. Writing down your challenges and how you handle them can create your own personal handbook of how to survive Anticipatory Grief.

Depending on how much time and ability to focus you have, starting a journal can provide an immediate outlet for your feelings as well as documenting sudden challenges you are facing. But don't just list what you are going through. Make a note of how you responded and what you did to ease your discomfort. Any relief, even temporary, is worth remembering for similar future issues. Many times, just the act of writing it down can be cathartic, helping you get it out of your mind (or heart) and move on with your day.

If "starting a journal" sounds too daunting in your current state of mind, just write short sentences or even phrases and hopefully a solution to look back on. Later when you face the same challenge, you can refresh your memory of what you did to ease the pain. You don't have to invest in a physical journal or notebook; you could keep this journal on your phone or computer so it can always be handy.

While writing down past solutions can help you while you move forward, so can making notes about what didn't work or how one single action started a series of cascading challenges. Knowing that trigger can also help you avoid that situation in the future. So, your journal can help you move forward from positive experiences and negative ones. Whatever information you need to help yourself in the future, make note of it and refer back to it often. This can really help - even if you're alone because you were there, and you understand yourself better than anyone else.

"Nutley and Tapawingo" has become a buzzword in my family, referring to situations that surprise us but leave us with something valuable learned about ourselves or those closest to us. We still mention and laugh about it today. Your journey through Anticipatory Grief can be the same way. While you tackle a specific challenge of Anticipatory Grief, journal about what you tried to take away from that experience, helping you remember what you discovered about yourself. Also keep in mind that Anticipatory Grief is an ongoing process, never knowing how long you will be in the tunnel. While you may work through one challenge, another may take its place. But with God's grace, you can survive this heartbreaking time.

The good news is that my sister quickly mastered the art of slowing down in anticipation of a turn. She is an excellent driver now. And while navigating the unpredictable journey of Anticipatory Grief, you can master it as well. When you encounter a new or even old challenge, refer to your journal and reflect on how you handled previous experiences. By doing this, you can help yourself while you learn to "do it right" next time.

6
BRAIN FOG

One of the greatest challenges you will face during Anticipatory Grief is brain fog. If you feel like your thinking has slowed to a crawl, if you have trouble remembering words or carrying on a coherent conversation, or if you can't seem to concentrate, these could be signs of brain fog. According to Miriam Webster, brain fog is "a usually temporary state of diminished mental capacity marked by inability to concentrate or to think or reason clearly."[20] While these sensations can make you doubt your sanity or cause you to set an appointment with your doctor, rest assured that many

Anticipatory Grief sufferers encounter these same challenges. But why is this happening?

This happens during Anticipatory Grief because the brain is handling so many other tasks that allowing you to think clearly is pushed to the background. Out of the countless neurons in the brain, only a fraction of around 10,000 to 20,000 secrete a neuropeptide known as orexin. Research indicates that this neuropeptide is part of a network responsible for keeping us awake and attentive. Fortunately, our brains are naturally wired to maintain a state of vigilance, enabling us to swiftly respond to our surroundings. However, this inherent clarity also sheds light on the disorienting and stressful nature of brain fog.[21]

Symptoms of Brain Fog

Brain fog is a collection of symptoms but not a medical term. These symptoms can include difficulty with concentration, confusion, slower thinking than usual, unclear thoughts, forgetfulness, struggling to find the right words, and mental fatigue. The sensation of brain fog can resemble the effects of sleep deprivation. It should be noted that brain fog is distinct from dementia and does not indicate any structural brain damage.[22] Generally, individuals tend to recover from brain fog as they deal with, and adapt to, Anticipatory Grief.

What are the effects of brain fog?

Brain fog can have negative effects on your usual creativity and productiveness at work. You may find it challenging to clear your desk with as much clarity as normal. If you find yourself missing deadlines or slogging through normally easy tasks, you might want to speak with your supervisor to clarify what you are going through. Depending on your relationship with your immediate supervisor, they might be understanding and allow you extra time to complete assignments.

Try not to get frustrated with yourself when you experience brain fog at work. You can always create a checklist for certain tasks, especially if they have many steps. You can also set reminders on your phone to let you know when a deadline is coming up so that you are not caught unprepared. Suffering through brain fog at work is the most frustrating type of brain fog because you are still expected to perform at your previous level.

Another effect of brain fog at work is a lower quality of work output. In the past you were probably performing your duties at 100% efficiency while now you might have days of working at 80% efficiency and even days at 20-40%. Know that this is normal with brain fog, and again, speaking with your immediate supervisor might help.

While some supervisors are less than understanding, this might not be a good option for you. In those situations, you could keep a journal of your work progress noting how you are feeling with a daily rating of your efficiency level. This would at least provide a document you could produce if your supervisor or others in charge asked you why your work was not up to its usual excellence.

Home is a bit more doable but still challenging. Your brain fog might prevent you from fulfilling household chores on your regular schedule. Buying groceries, paying bills, preparing meals, and washing dishes might seem overwhelming. If possible, maybe you could share the chores with other members of your family. But if the loved one for whom you are grieving in advance is a member of, or close to, your family, this might be even more challenging.

If you live with other people, having a weekly or twice weekly family huddle could ease some of your concern. If you live alone, don't be afraid to reach out to friends or loved ones to help you. Either way, sticky notes will be your new best friends. Use them for everything, and I mean everything. They will help you remember to do things but will also remind you that you have already done something. Add the date and time on each note so you know when it was written.

How can I treat and overcome brain fog?

Treating brain fog is not a one-size-fits-all approach due to various factors involved. However, you might want to try one or all of the following to ease the effects of brain fog on your daily life:

Take a break. Taking a break can be beneficial. Research suggests that stepping away from a task and giving yourself a momentary quit can improve performance, focus, and self-control. Certain activities like socializing, power napping, engaging in creativity, praying, and spending time outdoors can provide a more efficient break for your brain.

Watch your diet. Maintaining a balanced diet and incorporating foods high in antioxidants, such as blueberries and nuts, can positively impact brain health. Staying hydrated and including fish in your diet for omega-3 fatty acids is also important. When choosing healthy foods, be sure to find those that you enjoy. If you choose foods that you can barely tolerate, you won't be as motivated to eat them, negating this part of your plan.

Exercise. Exercise has been linked to improved brain function, pain relief, and emotional regulation. Various activities like walking, yoga, high-intensity exercises, stretching, and gardening can be beneficial. If you find it hard to motivate yourself to "get moving," you might consider volunteering to walk a neighbor's dog several mornings a week. The dog's family might appreciate a break, and you could make a new fur friend while motivating yourself to exercise.

Limit caffeine and alcohol consumption. They can impair cognitive function and cause symptoms of brain fog. If it's hard for you to limit your consumption of caffeine, try changing to a de-caffeinated drink or flavored water. If you like the taste, you will be more likely to choose the alternative, giving your brain a boost at the same time.

Get enough sleep. Prioritizing sleep by establishing a consistent sleep routine, avoiding stimulating substances, and creating a conducive sleep environment can significantly impact brain and overall health. If you check out YouTube, you can find many nature-focused sound effects that last as long as eight or more hours. Sounds such as thunderstorms, babbling brooks, night sounds, and ordinary "white noise" can help you relax and sleep better.[23]

If none of these solutions resonate with you, maybe they will spark similar ideas that will provide brain support. Since your brain is so important to your daily abilities, it's worth a little pondering to come up with something that will boost your brain's abilities.

My Prayer for You

Dear Heavenly Father,

I come before You with a heavy heart, seeking solace and strength for my dear friend who is grappling with Anticipatory Grief. Today, I bring a specific concern before You - the mental challenge of brain fog that often accompanies grief. I know that You are the God who brings clarity and understanding, even in times of confusion and pain.

Lord, I acknowledge that the brain fog of grief can cloud the mind and make it difficult to think clearly. It can hinder the ability to concentrate, make decisions, remember important details, and carry out daily tasks. I lift my friend, asking for Your mercy, grace, and healing touch upon their mental faculties.

In Your infinite wisdom, You created our minds to be sharp, focused, and capable of understanding. I pray that You will clear away the brain fog that hinders their mental clarity. Touch their mind, Lord, and grant them renewed sharpness of thought. Remove the obstacles that hinder their ability to think clearly, remember, and concentrate during this season of Anticipatory Grief.

Father, I ask for Your peace to descend upon my dear friend's mind. Calm any anxiety and restlessness that may contribute to the brain fog of Anticipatory Grief. Replace confusion with clarity, uncertainty with certainty, amnesia with memories, and chaos with calm. Grant them the ability to navigate through their thoughts with confidence and coherence.

Lord, I pray for strength and resilience in the face of brain fog. During times when it feels overwhelming, remind them of Your promise in Isaiah 40:31, that those who wait upon You will renew their strength. Help them to lean on You and rely on Your unfailing wisdom and guidance. May they find comfort in knowing that You are their source of strength in times of weakness.

Furthermore, Lord, I ask for understanding and empathy from those around them. Give their loved ones the sensitivity to offer support, patience, and care during this challenging season. Help them to recognize the impact of brain fog and extend grace and understanding in their interactions.

Ultimately, Heavenly Father, I surrender my friend and their struggle with brain fog to Your loving and capable hands. I trust that You have the power to restore clarity and bring forth peace. Surround them with Your unwavering love and reassure them that You are their refuge and strength in times of trouble.

In the mighty name of my Savior Jesus Christ, who understands every pain and struggle, I pray, Amen.

Support from The Word

Then He replied, "My presence will go with you, and I will give you rest." Exodus 33:14

The LORD is the One who will go before you. He will be with you; He will not leave you or forsake you. Do not be afraid or discouraged." Deuteronomy 31:8

I will both lie down and sleep in peace, for You alone, Lord, make me live in safety. Psalm 4:8

May He send you help from the sanctuary and sustain you from Zion. May He remember all your offerings and accept your burnt offering. May He give you what your heart desires and fulfill your whole purpose. Let us shout for joy at your victory and lift the banner in the name of your God. May Yahweh fulfill all your requests. Psalm 20:2-5

Therefore, my heart was glad, and my tongue rejoiced. Moreover, my flesh will rest in hope. Acts 2:26

7
Decision-Making Fatigue

According to Eva Krockow, lecturer at the University of Leicester in the United Kingdom, you make an average of 35,000 decisions in a normal day.[24] That's a lot of decisions, and most of them are made without any fanfare. But while you're in the Anticipatory Grief tunnel, decisions are monumentally challenging.

How anticipatory grief causes decision-making fatigue

You probably already realize that Anticipatory Grief negatively impacts decision making. Not only does it impair our ability to make new decisions, but it also disrupts brain chemistry, making it challenging to evaluate the pros and cons of choices, from choosing what to wear to deciding what to eat. But what is going on in our bodies during Anticipatory Grief, resulting in decision-making fatigue? The blood flow and oxygen to the brain decrease, creating a chaotic state that hinders access to crucial decision-making information. Consequently, decision making becomes compromised with risks sometimes outweighing potential rewards.[25]

Symptoms of Decision-making Fatigue

It might be surprising to realize that decision-making fatigue has more symptoms than just the inability to decide. It can also include:

Procrastinating frequently

Avoiding decision-making tasks

Exhibiting irritability and a short temper, often stemming from frustration with yourself

Acting impulsively

Feeling overwhelmed and potentially even hopeless

Spending excessive time deciding

Feeling a prevailing sense of dissatisfaction with any decision made, regardless of the choice

If you are experiencing one or several of these symptoms, you could be suffering from decision-making fatigue.[26]

Long-term Negative Effects of Decision-making Fatigue

Decision-making fatigue comes with several long-term effects. It can lead to poorer decision-making as you become more prone to making impulsive or irrational choices. It diminishes self-control and willpower. This can result in unhealthy habits, such as overeating, overspending, or having excessive screen time. Fatigue can impair risk assessment and increase the likelihood of engaging in risky behaviors. You tend to underestimate potential risks and make riskier choices due to depleted cognitive resources. It places a considerable cognitive load on you, leaving you mentally exhausted. Chronic fatigue can impact physical health by weakening the immune system and increasing vulnerability to illnesses. Mental exhaustion affects concentration, attention span, and overall performance, leading to decreased productivity and efficiency in completing tasks or making decisions. When you are subjected to decision-making fatigue, it can lead to increased irritability, impatience, and decreased empathy. This can strain personal relationships as you may be less understanding of the needs of others.

How to Work Through Decision-making Fatigue

To work through decision-making fatigue and avoid the long-term negative effects of it, try some or all the following strategies:

Make important decisions when the day begins. By making crucial choices early on, such as difficult phone calls or challenging tasks, you can set the stage for a more productive and profitable day. Knowing that your biggest challenges are completed should give you an emotional boost to feel better about yourself and set you up for a more successful day.

Simplify routine choices. Choose what you will wear the night before. Why not make a list of all your favorite and appropriate outfits, and then make a chart of when you will wear each one? With the chart in hand, you always know the night before just what you will need to have ready for the next day, avoiding the pressure of making the decision first thing in the morning when you have limited time.

Plan meals in advance. By creating a meal plan and preparing meals ahead of time, you can minimize decision-making pressure when it's time to eat. If you shop for groceries every other week, you could make a two-week meal plan and even know in advance what you would be making or reheating for dinner each night. This could save you time and even some money when shopping.

Take breaks throughout the day. Resting and recharging as needed, which may even include short naps, can help you make better decisions when they arise. If a short nap isn't possible, scope out a quiet, secluded spot (maybe in a lesser-used break room or a restroom with a small couch), and rest your eyes for 5-10 minutes. Don't think about work; just rest. Remember to set an alarm.[27]

Use lists to prioritize. Writing down tasks and decisions can help clear your mind and alleviate stress. By jotting down the top three tasks or decisions you need to make, you can stay focused, positive, and productive as you cross items off your list. Just in case you do something that isn't on your list, take a minute to add it to your list and then cross it off. Crossing out something that you didn't even have on your list originally can be a great mood-lifter.

Ask for advice. Making decisions on your own can be overwhelming and emotionally draining. It can be beneficial to reach out to a trusted friend, mentor, or family member when faced with difficult choices. Talking through your options together can provide support and guidance, particularly during Anticipatory Grief.

Prioritize self-care. It's crucial to make time for self-care during Anticipatory Grief. Engaging in activities, like taking a brisk walk outside or taking a midday nap, can recharge your energy for the rest of the day. Deep breathing exercises, stretching, and acknowledging your emotions can also give your brain a much-needed break. This way, you'll approach decision-making with a clearer mind and renewed energy. Take moments for mindfulness and adjust your daily habits to support your mental well-being.[28]

Sleep on it. Sleep not only refreshes your body, but it also refreshes your mind, which, in turn, can refresh your ability to make good decisions. Since you will probably make your most important decisions first thing in the morning, having a good night's sleep can give you time to subconsciously work through the decision.[29]

My Prayer for You

Dear Heavenly Father,

I come before You in humble submission, seeking Your comfort and guidance during a time of Anticipatory Grief. I recognize that You are the source of all wisdom and understanding. I acknowledge that decision-making fatigue can be overwhelming and burdensome, causing mental exhaustion and confusion. I ask that You come alongside my precious friend who is facing this challenge and provide them with the clarity and strength they need.

Lord, I know that You have promised to be with us in every season of life, including times of grief. I cling to Your Word which assures us of Your unfailing love and compassion. I trust in Your promises, knowing that You are faithful to fulfill them.

In times when decision making seems overwhelming, grant wisdom to my friend who is coping with Anticipatory Grief, Lord. Your word says that if any of us lack wisdom, we should ask You, and You will generously give it to us. We pray that You would specifically grant discernment to navigate through the complexities of decision-making fatigue. Help them to prioritize their thoughts and discern their options, and grant them the strength to make choices that align with Your will.

I pray for Your peace to flood their heart and mind. Help them to find rest and solace in Your presence. May Your Holy Spirit be their comforter and guide, guiding their mind as they make both routine and difficult decisions.

Lord, I also pray for the support of their loved ones, friends, and church community during this time. Help them to surround themselves with people who can provide empathy, encouragement, and practical assistance. May they receive love and understanding as they face the mental fatigue that accompanies Anticipatory Grief.

Father, I know that You understand every burden we carry. You are acquainted with our sorrows and pains. So, I lay these burdens before You, knowing that Your love and care for us is boundless. I trust in Your promise to sustain my dear friend and give them peace that surpasses all understanding.

I ask all these things in the name of our Lord and Savior, Jesus Christ, who I know is our ultimate source of comfort and strength, Amen.

Support from The Word

I will instruct you and teach you in the way you should go; I will counsel you with my loving eye on you. Psalm 32:8

Commit to the LORD whatever you do, and He will establish your plans. Proverbs 16:3

Whether you turn to the right or to the left, your ears will hear a voice behind you, saying, "This is the way; walk in it." Isaiah 30:21

Do not conform to the pattern of this world but be transformed by the renewing of your mind. Then you will be able to test and approve what God's will is—his good, pleasing, and perfect will. Romans 12:2

If any of you lacks wisdom, you should ask God, who gives generously to all without finding fault, and it will be given to you. James 1:5

8
Problem Solving

Anticipatory Grief can have significant effects on the brain. One common symptom is known as Grief Brain, which can cause the inability to solve problems and difficulty expressing thoughts. While these effects are typically temporary, they can be distressing.

For some people, Anticipatory Grief may last six months to a year, depending on the severity of the loved one's diagnosis and speed of the illness's progression. During this time, it can be difficult to solve problems.

8 Problem Solving | 73

The brain reacts to Anticipatory Grief similarly to how it handles stress. Prolonged Anticipatory Grief can put the brain in a state of chronic stress, leading to various physiological responses. Fight-or-flight hormones are released, heart rate increases, and blood flow shifts towards more emotional and fear-based regions of the brain, rather than the areas associated with higher-level thinking. The prefrontal cortex, responsible for problem solving, becomes less active, while the limbic system, responsible for survival instincts, takes over.

Depending on the intensity of the Anticipatory Grief response, the brain starts rewiring its neural connections, reinforcing emotional and fear-based thoughts while potentially challenging long-held beliefs. Reminders of the loved one's imminent passing can trigger this stress response and further strengthen these new pathways.

Over time, Anticipatory Grief can impact attention, memory, decision-making, verbal expression, information-processing speed, and cognitive functions reliant on movement and depth perception. Overall, Anticipatory Grief not only affects our emotional state but also has profound consequences on brain function.[30]

Symptoms of problem-solving challenges

Megan Devine, psychotherapist and author, explains Grief Brain like this: "If you think of the mind as having 100 circuits of energy, grief takes up 99 of those. Grief is like your brain turning this information over and over and over and trying to find a place where it fits. It's not going to fit, but your mind is trying to make it so. It's trying to make this story work out in a way that is acceptable. How do you make this death acceptable? You can't, but your brain's working on it, which means that you have one unit of energy left for everything else."[31]

Realizing that you only have a tiny bit of brain function left to cope with your life, it's easy to understand why problem solving is so challenging. Add to that the fact that Anticipatory Grief can affect your perception of time, and you have a major hurdle to overcome.

Symptoms of problem-solving challenges can include:
Difficulties in controlling emotions or impulses
Difficulties in initiating or finishing tasks
Challenges in listening
Issues with short-term memory
Trouble multitasking or balancing multiple tasks
Exhibiting socially inappropriate behavior[32]

Consequences of inability to solve problems

While you are maneuvering the twists and turns of the Anticipatory Grief tunnel, problem-solving challenges can interrupt several key areas of your life.

At work, depending on your position and responsibilities, your job could include solving many problems a day, whether for those you supervise, your peers, or those to whom you report. Without the ability to make recommendations for ways to solve a problem, your authority could be jeopardized, and your opinion questioned or even doubted.

At home, things might be a bit easier, but you could still experience challenges on a more personal level. If your child asks permission for something, and you are not ready or able to discuss the issue with your partner, you might end up disagreeing, which could escalate into a more serious issue. Or you might be called on to solve a plumbing issue and "freeze," making it difficult for someone to take action to remedy the issue.

How to combat the inability to solve problems

Dealing with problems comes in all shapes and sizes, from your car not starting to a debit card that won't work. Normally dealing with these types of issues is no problem. But during Anticipatory Grief, using the executive functions that include problem solving can make problems become much larger. The problems you need to solve each day at work pile on even more challenges.

Here are some ways to combat and overcome problem-solving issues:

Practice self-care. Ensure you are getting sufficient rest, maintaining a nutritious diet, and setting aside moments for relaxation. Avoid resorting to alcohol or recreational drugs as a means of finding relief. For more detailed recommendations about self-care, read the Self-Care Chapter in the Relational Part of this book.

Exercise regularly. It doesn't have to be a full 60-minute heavy cardio workout. So, do what works for you, and ensure you enjoy it enough to practice it at least two to two and a half hours a week. It doesn't have to be strenuous exercise; it just needs to be something that makes you move. Walking, stretching, dancing, or anything that you enjoy can be a way to exercise.

Journal. Writing down disturbing memories or dreams can help you become more aware of unprocessed thoughts, memories, and emotions. Also writing down happy memories, laughs shared with your loved one, and favorite remembrances can provide a lighter mood and clarity of thought.

Meditate or pray. Practicing mindfulness and relaxation can be outlets for releasing stress and allowing peace and calm to saturate your mind. Problem solving is easier when your mind is in a happy and peaceful place. Even if you don't have to solve a problem right now, maintaining this practice can keep you in a good mental place for future problem solving.

Get support. Talking about your feelings, even at the most difficult times, can help diminish the inability to solve problems. It can be helpful to talk to a person outside the family, such as a counselor or trusted friend. If you are a caregiver and temporarily residing close to your loved one and away from your normal friends, you can still speak with them by phone or text. If a time change interferes with a good time to speak on the phone, you could look for a local counselor who uses video appointments.

Use Cognitive Behavioral Therapy (CBT). CBT is a common form of therapy for conditions caused by executive function issues like decision making or problem solving. The main aim of CBT is to help you take a fresh look at your own perspectives and thinking patterns so you can gain better control over your behavior. The idea is to empower you with the tools and skills needed to make positive changes in your life.[33]

My Prayer for You

Dear Heavenly Father,

I come before You today with a heavy heart, seeking Your comfort and guidance for my precious friend who is coping with Anticipatory Grief. I lift them up to You, knowing that You are the source of all peace, strength, and healing.

Lord, I acknowledge that the difficulties of life can often overwhelm us, especially when we feel helpless in solving our problems. I ask that You surround my dear friend with Your loving presence and grant them clarity of mind during this time of Anticipatory Grief. Help them to trust in Your perfect timing and plan, even when they are unable to find solutions to their problems.

Lord, remind them that You are the ultimate problem-solver and that nothing is too difficult for You. I pray for Your wisdom to fill their mind, guiding them to seek Your will in each situation they face. Strengthen their faith and remind them that You are always in control, even when their circumstances may seem overwhelming.

In moments of doubt, help them to turn to You in prayer, offering up their concerns and anxieties. Teach them to cast their burdens upon You, for You care for them deeply. Let Your Holy Spirit provide them with peace that surpasses all understanding, guarding their hearts and minds in Christ Jesus.

Lord, surround them with a supportive community of believers who can provide encouragement and companionship during this challenging time. May they find solace in the fellowship of other believers who can remind them of Your faithfulness and offer loving counsel as they face their struggles. May they ask for, and receive, Godly advice on how to solve specific problems they face and give them the openness and willingness to accept "wise counsel" from their faithful brothers and sisters.

Finally, I ask for Your comfort to envelop my dear friend as they navigate through this Anticipatory Grief. Remind them of Your promise in Isaiah 41:10, that You are with them and Your strong hand will uphold them. Grant them patience, perseverance, and hope as they lean on You for strength and understanding.

I trust in Your unfailing love and faithfulness, O Lord, knowing that You have conquered death through the resurrection of Your Son, Jesus Christ.

In His name, I pray, Amen.

Support from The Word

Cast your cares on the Lord and He will sustain you; He will never let the righteous be shaken. Psalm 55:22

Teach me Your way, Yahweh, and I will live by Your truth. Give me an undivided mind to fear Your name. Psalm 86:11

Come to me, all you who are weary and burdened, and I will give you rest. Take My yoke upon you and learn from me, for I am gentle and humble in heart, and you will find rest for your souls. For My yoke is easy and My burden is light. Matthew 11:28-30

My grace is sufficient for you, for My power is made perfect in weakness. Therefore, I will boast all the more gladly about my weaknesses, so that Christ's power may rest on me. 2 Corinthians 12:9

Do not be anxious about anything, but in every situation, by prayer and petition, with thanksgiving, present your requests to God. And the peace of God, which transcends all understanding, will guard your hearts and your minds in Christ Jesus. Philippians 4:6-7

9
Lack of Motivation

Lack of motivation is one of the most common problems that people face during Anticipatory Grief. The feeling of not wanting to do anything or putting off tasks is a legitimate concern. Whether it is delaying the start of a project, avoiding a difficult conversation, or procrastinating on a significant task, it can be a huge mental challenge.

What Are the symptoms of lack of motivation?

Lack of motivation or low motivation experienced during Anticipatory Grief displays some of the same symptoms as laziness. But Anticipatory Grief can make it hard to pinpoint what you are going through. So how can you tell where you are on the slippery slope of motivation? The following distinctions should help.

Laziness is a choice, a desire to do nothing and enjoy the nothingness. Sometimes, taking a day off to relax is perfectly fine. But when laziness affects daily tasks, it has a different effect. You have the desire but lack the willingness to put in the effort. Instead of doing nothing, you find shortcuts in order to get things done quickly. Quality isn't a concern as long as the work is finished. You would rather have someone else do the work and prefer unproductive tasks. Procrastination is your specialty, and you prioritize what you want over what is required.

Lack of motivation, on the other hand, stems from a lack of passion. There are no goals, desires, or willingness to work. You simply "can't" or don't do anything; there is no pretending like laziness. Your lack of motivation is a response to your current situation, Anticipatory Grief. Over time, this leads to losing any passion you may have once had. You appreciate progress but just aren't feeling it right now. You dislike things that don't bring any benefits. Being a perfectionist can also lead to procrastination. You procrastinate because you have no interest in the project and engage in unproductive behavior as a means of escape, not enjoyment. However, you become hardworking when motivated.[34]

In case the previous two paragraphs were a bit fuzzy, the takeaway from this chapter is this: You are NOT lazy. Lack of motivation is caused by your Anticipatory Grief, and you can do something about it.

The different manifestations of lack of motivation

Lack of motivation comes in all shapes and sizes. While one person might be unmotivated because they feel like they're too tired, you might feel as if the task is too hard. Remember, just because you feel a task is too hard today doesn't mean your lack of motivation will manifest in that same way tomorrow.

The following list contains an excuse and what to do about it:

I'll do it later. Setting clear priorities can help.

I don't feel like it. Creating a schedule and establishing consistency can help.

It's too hard. This is probably the truest statement. Breaking tasks down into smaller, more manageable steps can help.

I'm too tired. Prioritizing sleep, exercising, and praying can help.

It doesn't matter. Setting specific goals and developing a clear vision of the future can help.

I'll never get it done. Focusing on the present or seeking support from friends, family, or a therapist can help.

This is all my fault. Practicing self-compassion and self-reflection can help.

I don't have the inspiration. Changing up your environment or routine and experimenting with new or different ways of doing things can help.[35]

How to regain motivation

When we compare ourselves with others, it seems like they have motivation to spare. They effortlessly jump out of bed, ready to conquer the world. Meanwhile, when you're going through Anticipatory Grief, just getting out of bed, or doing something that would make you feel better feels like an uphill battle.

Here's the thing. We often believe that these world-conquerors were motivated before they even started moving, but it's actually the opposite. We feel motivated because of our past successes. So, if our recent experiences have been failures, it's only natural not to feel motivated. Instead of waiting around for motivation to magically appear, let's focus on building momentum.

Building momentum is like pushing a giant rock downhill. First, you need to pick a direction. Making small movements in every direction won't get you anywhere. Concentrate on making small movements in the direction you want to go. When you're feeling like you are right now, every ounce of your brain and body resists any kind of movement. That's why it's important to start with small changes.

But here's another key element. Set a direction for yourself. Ask yourself, "Where do I want to go?" Then, take the smallest step in that direction. Let's say you've decided to lose weight. "Weight loss" is a giant, vague goal that can feel overwhelming. So, let's break it down. Start by choosing one healthy meal to try out. It may seem like a tiny change, but trust me, it builds momentum. And the more momentum you have, the easier it becomes to make further changes, like going to the store to buy the ingredients for that meal.

Now, I want you to pay attention to something important. Your brain is constantly evaluating what's happening around you and drawing conclusions. The problem is, even though your thoughts may seem logical and accurate, they're as influenced by external circumstances as your behaviors are. In other words, the negative thoughts you're having, like "I'll never achieve anything" or "I can't do this," are a direct result of the tough times you're going through. But here's the truth. Those thoughts aren't honest, true, or rational.

To change these negative thoughts, you need to dismiss them and change your situation. So, how do you change your situation? By building momentum. As you start changing the behaviors associated with Anticipatory Grief, your thoughts will naturally follow suit and become more positive, accurate, and rational. So, when you try out that weight loss meal, your brain will have less room to say, "I'll never lose weight" and more room for positive, rational thoughts. Remember, it's a gradual process, so take your time, make small changes, and celebrate every single success, no matter how small.[36]

Once that giant rock starts rolling downhill, your momentum will lead to motivation, and your motivation will lead to getting things done. They might be small things, but small things lead to bigger things. So, celebrate every step of the journey to being motivated again.

My Prayer for You

Dear Heavenly Father,

I come before You with a heavy heart, seeking Your divine guidance and comfort for my precious friend who is coping with Anticipatory Grief. I lift their burdened soul to You, knowing that You are the ultimate source of strength and solace.

Lord, I recognize that the mental toll of Anticipatory Grief can lead to a lack of motivation, making it difficult for my friend to navigate through their daily struggles. I ask for Your presence to surround them, bringing renewed energy and purpose to their weary spirit.

Grant them clarity of mind and peace that surpasses all understanding. Help them to find motivation in knowing that You are ever-present, guiding their steps and providing comfort in their time of need. Open their hearts to the assurance that their grief is not in vain, but that it is a testament to the love they have for their loved one.

May the truth of Your Word, the Bible, fill their thoughts and renew their perspective. Remind them of the promises You have given us, that You have a better plan for our lives than we could ever imagine. Help them to rely on Your wisdom and trust in Your leadership, especially when motivation seems distant and difficult to grasp.

Lord, in their moments of weakness, where the burdens of Anticipatory Grief overwhelm their spirit, may they turn to You in prayer. Help them to lay their burdens at Your feet, knowing that You are a God who listens and responds. May the language of prayer be their refuge and the means by which they find solace and clarity.

Through their journey of Anticipatory Grief, let them experience the closeness of Jesus, the resurrected Son of God. Remind them that Jesus understands their pain and sorrow, having experienced His own anticipation of the cross. May Your Son's example of obedience and surrender inspire them to press on even when motivation wanes.

Dear Lord, I ask for Your loving presence to surround my dear friend each day. May they feel Your love in every moment and find comfort in knowing that You are their Heavenly Father, eager to uplift and support them. Help them to embrace Your unfailing love, permeating their thoughts and replacing any doubts or fears.

In the midst of their Anticipatory Grief, guide them to find joy in Your provision for their needs. Help them to recognize the blessings that surround them, even during their pain. Remind them that You are a God of abundance and that Your provision extends beyond their material needs to the healing of their heart.

Father, grant them the ability to awake each morning with motivation to accomplish great things for You. Give them clarity of thought and the ability to organize the steps they need to follow to reach their goals.

Lastly, Lord, I ask for Your divine protection over my dear friend. Shield them from the enemy's lies and attacks that seek to steal their hope and motivation. Surround them with a community of fellow believers who can walk alongside them, providing support and encouragement through this difficult time.

I thank you, Lord, for hearing my prayer, and I trust that You will answer according to your perfect will. In the powerful name of Jesus, I pray, Amen.

Support from The Word

Commit your way to the LORD, trust in Him, and He will act. Psalm 37:5

Commit to the LORD whatever you do, and He will establish your plans. Proverbs 16:3

Let us not become weary in doing good, for at the proper time we will reap a harvest if we do not give up. Galatians 6:9

I can do all things through Christ who strengthens me. Philippians 4:13

Whatever you do, work at it with all your heart, as working for the Lord, not for human masters, since you know that you will receive an inheritance from the Lord as a reward. It is the Lord Christ you are serving. Colossians 3:23-24

10
Loneliness

Loneliness is that feeling we get when we're missing out on the companionship we desire. It's subjective and definitely not something we welcome. Basically, it's when the number and quality of our relationships don't quite measure up to what we really want or need. Occasionally, we all experience loneliness, whether we're surrounded by people or not. It's just the way our minds and emotions process what we are experiencing.

During Anticipatory Grief, whether you are a caregiver or not, your attention is so focused on your loved one and your uncertain future without them, you may tend to withdraw from normal social situations. While the solitude can be comforting at the moment, this lack of social interaction can lead to loneliness, causing a bit of a Catch 22 situation. If possible, scheduling socialization with people you trust can help prevent or alleviate the loneliness you're experiencing.

Various forms of loneliness exist, three of which have been extensively studied and documented in evidence and literature. First, there is Emotional Loneliness, which refers to the lack of meaningful relationships. Second, Social Loneliness is characterized by perceiving a deficiency in the quality of social connections. Lastly, Existential Loneliness entails experiencing a profound sense of isolation and detachment from others and the broader world.[37]

During a period of Anticipatory Grief in my life, I experienced both Social and Existential Loneliness more than Emotional Loneliness. Your experience might be similar. Social Loneliness will cause you to be lonely for people, experiences, your loved one, your loved one's previous health, and the relationship you once shared. Existential Loneliness is a bit more subtle but could manifest in stronger ways. This loneliness leaves you feeling isolated from the rest of the world because they don't always understand why you are feeling the way you are and how they can help. You might even be lonely for the future since it is now different. Some of these things might sound odd, but they do happen. You might have already experienced this a bit but had trouble putting a name on what you were experiencing.

While I was going through Anticipatory Grief, I called this "feeling homeless" because I felt I had no ties to anyone or anything. You might describe it differently, but if you analyze it a bit more deeply, you may recognize it as loneliness.

Symptoms of loneliness

Because men and woman are different and approach life differently, the loneliness symptoms they manifest are slightly different.

Despite the scientific evidence indicating that loneliness is prevalent among men, many choose to avoid discussing their loneliness to avoid being seen as "weak" by others. Consequently, the symptoms of loneliness in men may appear differently from what is typically associated with loneliness. It is crucial to understand that loneliness can manifest as aggression, avoidance, or engagement in risky behavior in men. Instead of openly expressing their loneliness, men may turn to substances, such as alcohol, to numb their feelings or exhibit increased agitation towards minor issues. Men have been socialized to display fewer emotions in general, and recognizing this can help interpret the signs of loneliness in men.

Studies have indicated that women are more likely to report experiencing loneliness compared to men. Additionally, research has shown that women with fewer close relationships are more prone to feelings of loneliness. Consequently, the signs of loneliness in women often involve openly expressing their sense of isolation and the challenges they face in establishing deep connections with others. Some women, particularly those considered "too" attractive by their female peers, may feel excluded from social activities or workplace cliques, leading to feelings of isolation. Women may turn to social media as a coping mechanism, despite its link to increased levels of loneliness. Instead of feeling connected, excessive use of social media may exacerbate their feelings of isolation. Lonely women often struggle with negative self-perception, which has been associated with overall life dissatisfaction. This can manifest as restlessness or uneasiness in their daily lives.[38]

How to overcome loneliness

While Anticipatory Grief loneliness can sometimes be an underlying symptom, it is still important to address and overcome. Although you may not feel like reaching out, do the best you can to break free from your loneliness.

Hopefully, one of the following ideas will interest you:

Reach out. Work on improving your communication skills and reach out to trusted friends for more social contact. Schedule regular contact with family to ask about their lives and share recent events. Plan structured outings or activities with friends to stay connected. If your schedule allows, take a day trip to explore a place you both have always wanted to go. Enjoy a weekly walk with a friend or acquaintance to get to know them better.

Branch out. If you feel stuck, loneliness can be alleviated by trying something new. Engaging in a new hobby not only introduces you to a community with similar interests but also adds excitement to your daily life and enhances your self-esteem. You could take a class at a community college or join a club focused on something you enjoy, such as reading, gardening, or travel. You could even volunteer to help at a senior center, Meals on Wheels®, or your local library or hospital.

Reduce social media time. It would seem that social media would be a great place to interact with people since you can easily reach out to people through messages. But when you are lonely, especially during Anticipatory Grief, posting or messaging on social media can actually make you lonelier by seeing others engaging in happy times. Instead, replace your social media time with something that brings you joy, such as engaging in a hobby, singing, or listening to music.

Find a support group. Joining a support group can be an excellent way to meet new people who understand exactly what you are going through. Options such as What'sYourGrief.org, GriefShare, or organizations focused on the illness of your loved one can provide online or face-to-face support groups where you can share your feelings and get to know other people in similar situations. If you find a grief support group, you should still not hesitate to join just because you are experiencing Anticipatory Grief rather than traditional grief.

Willfully receive. If you are a giver or a helper, you know what it feels like to give. But sometimes givers are not always comfortable receiving. When someone offers to help you, it can be easier to say you don't need anything or "I'm fine." But responding in that way can deprive them of the gift of helping. Be willing to accept someone's offer of kindness, whether food, a phone call, or an in-person visit. Your acceptance of their kindness might be a real blessing in their day.

My Prayer for You

Dear Heavenly Father,

I humbly come before You, aware of the deep sorrow and loneliness that weighs heavily on the heart of my dear friend who is coping with Anticipatory Grief. Lord, You are the compassionate One Who understands the depths of emotions and the ache of longing for companionship. Today, I specifically lift the mental area of loneliness in their life.

Father, I acknowledge that the anticipation of losing a loved one can bring a profound sense of isolation and emptiness. The impending absence of their presence can create a void that feels unbearable. In these moments, I ask for Your comfort and understanding to flood their minds and hearts.

Lord, I pray that You, in Your boundless love, surround my friend with Your presence. Bridge the gap of loneliness and bring them a deep sense of comfort and connection. May they discover comfort in knowing that You are with them, even in their deepest moments of despair.

Father, I ask for You to provide them with compassionate and understanding companions who can walk alongside them during this season of Anticipatory Grief. Surround them with loving individuals who will offer a listening ear, a caring heart, and a comforting presence. Shine Your light on those who can lift their spirits and bring a sense of belonging to their lives.

Lord, I pray for strength and resilience in the face of loneliness. Help my friend to find solace in Your words in Joshua 1:9, that You are always with us and will never leave us nor forsake us. Empower them to draw close to You, finding comfort and companionship in the depth of their relationship with You.

Father, I ask that You grant them the ability to cherish and hold dear the memories of togetherness with their loved one. Strengthen their mind and heart to recall the moments of joy, laughter, and connection they once shared. Remind them that even in the absence of physical presence, the bond they shared still resides within their heart.

Lastly, Lord, I pray for Your divine provision to fill any void left by loneliness. Help my precious friend to find purpose and meaning in serving others, in reaching out to those who may also be feeling isolated, and in leaning into their faith community for support. May they experience the beauty of the body of Christ, finding fellowship and kinship in their fellow believers.

Father, I entrust my dear friend and their journey of coping with Anticipatory Grief to Your tender care. Hug them up in Your loving embrace and grant them the strength to face each day with hope and trust in Your unfailing love.

In the precious name of Jesus, who understands my every sorrow and never leaves us alone, I pray, Amen.

Support from The Word

LORD, You have searched me and known me. You know when I sit down and when I stand up; You understand my thoughts from far away. You observe my travels and my rest; You are aware of all my ways. Before a word is on my tongue, You know all about it, LORD. You have encircled me; You have placed Your hand on me. Psalm 139:1-5

The LORD is near all who call out to Him, all who call out to Him with integrity. Psalm 145:18

A man with many friends may be harmed, but there is a friend who stays closer than a brother. Proverbs 18:24

What then are you to say about these things? If God is for us, who is against us? Romans 8:31

The Lord will rescue me from every evil work and will bring me safely into His heavenly kingdom. To Him be the glory forever and ever! Amen. 2 Timothy 4:18

Part 3
Physical Challenges

> Anticipatory grief drains you of your energy, leaving you with a heavy burden of fatigue, and even the simplest things become insurmountable challenges, slogging through the slime of sadness. – Cindi Dawson

The summer after my freshman year of college, my family moved from Texas to Virginia when my dad was transferred. But my sister and I were still going to school in Texas. I was getting my bachelor's degree, and my older sister was getting her master's. For us to spend the summer with my family, we chose to save some money and drive the 1,500-mile trip. And that's when it started.

I'm one of those people who is always hot. And my sister is one of those normal people who enjoys normal temperatures. So, it was no surprise when, a couple of hours into the trek, I became increasingly uncomfortable. We had the air conditioner on, but that did little to ease my discomfort. I tried to ignore it, focusing on the songs we heard on the radio. But my body was complaining, and finally I realized I needed to bring it up.

As you are proceeding through the Anticipatory Grief tunnel, your experience will be unique. This could be the first time you have ever experienced so many different sensations at the same time. But if you are keeping a journal while traveling through the tunnel, as mentioned in the introduction to Part 2 Mental Challenges, you will notice a pattern. Most of your symptoms might be physical, emotional, or mental. That isn't good or bad; it's just you. All is well. You have no need to be embarrassed or singled out. Your body is doing what everyone else's body is doing. It's just different.

I asked my sister if she was hot, and, of course, she wasn't. So, I politely asked if we could turn down the air conditioner temperature to make it a bit cooler. Being the wonderful, understanding, and loving sister that she was (and still is), she complied and turned the thermostat cooler. A few minutes later, she reached into the back seat and grabbed something to put over her legs since she was wearing shorts. And the trip continued, crisis averted.

When God created us, He made us all different, including identical twins. According to Dr. Claire Asher at the University of Leeds, even though identical twins share the same DNA sequence and usually bear a striking resemblance, their fingerprints still display slight variations. This is due to the combination of genetic and environmental influences that shape the development of fingerprints in the womb.[39]

There is no right or wrong way to survive the Anticipatory Grief tunnel. Rest in the knowledge that you are handling your emotions, cognitive functions, and physical symptoms the best you can, and that says a great deal about your resilience.

As my sister and I continued down the road, I was getting hotter by the minute, even with the air conditioner temperature lowered. So, I asked again if we could turn down the air conditioner, and to my surprise, she agreed. But after lowering the temperature yet again, she reached into the back seat and produced a sweater! Then she announced, "OK, I'm all set now. The temperature is in your hands." We both laughed, and that's how we both arrived at the same destination in totally opposite ways. The road was the same, the car was the same, the rest stops were the same, but the clothing was all different.

Your Anticipatory Grief journey will be different, but you will change, grow, and learn a lot about yourself as you take one step at a time. Rejoice in the fact that you are unique and will have a unique story to tell as you emerge on the other side of the Anticipatory Grief tunnel.

11
Insomnia

Sleep is an essential part of your overall well-being, and getting enough quality sleep is critical to your health and productivity. However, sleep can be a challenge, and sleep disturbances can be frustrating and debilitating, especially during periods of intense and prolonged stress or anxiety, such as Anticipatory Grief. In order to cope with, and overcome, your Anticipatory Grief symptoms, sleep is more important than ever.

How close you are to your loved one can contribute greatly to the severity of your sleep problems. Anticipatory Grief has an impact on physical health, worsening sleep issues and intensifying the anticipatory grieving process. For instance, approximately 43% of grieving individuals experience a loss of appetite. The anticipated loss of a loved one often brings significant lifestyle changes, such as less physical activity and social interaction, both of which can negatively affect sleep. Sedentary lifestyles and feelings of loneliness alone are predictors of poor sleep.[40]

Insomnia is probably the most common sleep disturbance. You have probably experienced insomnia at some time in your life, whether for one night or over several nights or even weeks. Insomnia is when you have trouble falling asleep or staying asleep. Then if you wake in the middle of the night, it is difficult to get back to sleep, even if you can. Insomnia can make your night's sleep more exhausting than helpful. When this happens several nights in a row, your days are less productive and can be challenging.[41]

The biggest negative effect of insomnia is excessive sleepiness during the day. Sleepiness can make you irritable and cause you to have a lower-than-normal ability to solve problems or make decisions. Any one of these side effects could cause challenges at work.

How can I get to sleep right now?

Figuring out how to prevent insomnia or any other type of sleep disturbance from hindering a good night's sleep in the future is all well and good, but what can you do right this minute when your brain won't stop, memories or worries keep playing over and over in your mind, and you need a good, sound night's sleep? Here are a few recommendations that I tried. Some of them helped me while navigating the Anticipatory Grief tunnel.

The first technique is a brain dump. Grab your notetaking app or an old-fashioned piece of paper and a pen (Everyone is different.) to jot down any lingering thoughts or concerns that may be keeping you awake. Don't try to solve these issues. Just jot them down. By putting these thoughts onto paper, you can clear your mind and alleviate any worries that may be keeping you awake.

Breathing exercises are another effective technique for inducing sleep. Slow, deep breathing can help lower your heart rate and relax your body. One effective technique is the 4-7-8 method, where you inhale for a count of four, hold your breath for seven, and exhale for eight. This one was especially helpful for me.

The sounds of nature have a soothing effect on the mind and body. Whether it's the sound of rainfall, ocean waves, or a gentle breeze, these natural sounds can create a calm environment conducive to sleep. There are numerous apps and websites available that provide a variety of nature sound effects to choose from.

Coloring is not just for children; it can also be a relaxing activity for adults. Engaging in coloring before bed or when you can't sleep can help shift your focus away from any stressful thoughts and promote a sense of calmness. Choose intricate designs and soothing colors to enhance the relaxation effect.

Warm milk has long been considered a natural sleep aid. The amino acid, tryptophan, present in milk helps increase melatonin levels, promoting relaxation and a more restful sleep. Sipping on a warm glass of milk can be a soothing and comforting routine.

Similarly, chamomile tea is well-known for its calming properties. This herbal tea is believed to have mild sedative effects and can help reduce anxiety and promote sleep. Brew a cup of chamomile tea and enjoy its warmth and fragrance to help you wind down for the night.

Progressive muscle relaxation is a technique that involves tensing and releasing different muscle groups, promoting a sense of relaxation throughout the body. Start by tensing and releasing the muscles in your toes, and gradually work your way up to your head. This technique can help alleviate physical tension that may be interfering with your sleep.

Prayer or meditation can be powerful tools in quieting the mind and promoting a sense of peace. Engaging in a prayer or meditation practice before bed can help you let go of any remaining stress or worries, allowing your mind to enter a more tranquil state conducive to sleep.

Taking a warm bath before bed can aid in relaxation. The warm water promotes muscle relaxation and can help lower your body temperature, signaling to your brain that it's time to sleep. Incorporate calming essential oils, such as lavender or chamomile, for an added sleep-inducing effect.

Yoga or gentle stretching can be an excellent way to relax both the mind and body before bed. Engaging in a few simple stretches or gentle yoga poses can help release any physical tension built up throughout the day, preparing your body for a restful night's sleep.

Lastly, utilizing a guided meditation app specifically designed for sleep can be highly effective. These apps provide a variety of calming and soothing recordings that guide you into a state of relaxation, making it easier to transition into a restful sleep.

How to improve your sleep in the future

It can be challenging to achieve restful sleep during Anticipatory Grief. The first step is to be understanding and patient with yourself if you're having trouble sleeping. Give yourself grace during this difficult time.

Once you feel ready, consider trying these tips to help you get more rest and improve your overall sleep quality

Establish a routine. While enduring Anticipatory Grief, your daily schedule may not be the same as before. However, creating a predictable pattern for eating, sleeping, and daily activities can promote better sleep.

Set a bedtime. Incorporate a consistent bedtime and wake time into your new routine, even if you didn't sleep well the night before. This will help your body establish a natural sleep-wake cycle, making it easier to feel tired and fall asleep at the same time each night and wake at the same time each morning.

Eliminate distractions. Remove any distractions from your bedroom that may interfere with sleep, such as a television or smartphone. The charging message on your smartphone can disrupt your sleep.

Create a sleep-friendly environment. Optimize your bedroom for sleep by using blackout curtains to make the room dark, using a white noise machine to drown out external noises, keeping the room at a comfortable, cool temperature, and ensuring good ventilation for a comfortable sleep environment.

Engage in regular exercise. Although it may not be your top priority during the Anticipatory Grief process, including daily physical activity like walking can help you fall asleep more easily at night. Avoid exercising immediately before bedtime, as it may have a stimulating effect.

Watch your diet. Avoid consuming large meals, alcohol, and caffeine close to bedtime, as they can interfere with sleep. Consider enjoying a cup of tea to help you relax, but be mindful that it may cause nighttime bathroom visits.[42]

My Prayer for You

Dear Heavenly Father,

In this moment, I come before You with a heart heavy with Anticipatory Grief, seeking Your comforting presence for my dear friend who is grappling with the physical challenge of insomnia. Lord, You are the ultimate source of peace and rest, and I humbly ask for Your touch upon their body and mind during this time of turmoil.

Father, I acknowledge that Anticipatory Grief can disrupt sleep patterns, leading to restless nights and weariness in my friend's physical body. I lift this struggle to You, knowing that You can bring restoration and healing even during sleeplessness.

Lord, I ask for Your divine intervention in promoting restful sleep for my beloved friend. Grant them the ability to find peace and tranquility as they lay down to rest. Calm any anxious thoughts or worries that may be plaguing their mind, and replace them with a deep sense of peace and trust in Your loving care.

Father, I pray for a release of tension within their body. Relieve any physical discomfort or pain that may hinder their ability to sleep. Restore their body's natural rhythm and balance, creating an environment conducive to deep and restorative sleep. Bring healing to their body, mind, and soul, allowing them to wake up rejuvenated and ready to face each new day.

Lord, I ask for Your strengthening grace for my friend, particularly during those moments when sleep eludes them. Uphold them in their weariness, guarding their health and well-being. Grant them the physical stamina needed to navigate the challenges of each day, despite the lack of sleep.

Infuse their body with renewed energy and vitality, enabling them to focus and function to the best of their abilities.

Father, I pray for their mind to find rest even in the wakefulness of night. Help them to channel their thoughts towards You, finding comfort and peace in Your presence. Reassure them of Your constant companionship, even in the silent hours of the night, as they turn their worries and burdens over to You in prayer.

Lastly, Lord, I pray for Your wisdom to guide them in their approach to managing insomnia. Lead them to seek appropriate medical and professional help if necessary, that they may find tangible solutions and strategies to promote better sleep. Surround them with a support system that offers understanding and encouragement throughout their journey.

Father, I entrust my dear friend and their struggle with insomnia to Your compassionate care. Surround them with Your love and fill their nights with restful sleep. Grant them the strength to face each day with courage and resilience, knowing that You are their refuge and strength.

In the name of Jesus Christ, my Great Comforter, I pray, Amen.

Support from The Word

I lie down and sleep; I wake again because the Lord sustains me. Psalm 3:5

I will both lie down and sleep in peace, for You alone, Lord, make me live in safety. Psalm 4:8

You will keep the mind that is dependent on You in perfect peace, for it is trusting in You. Isaiah 26:3

"Though the mountains move and the hills shake, My love will not be removed from you and My covenant of peace will not be shaken," says your compassionate Lord. Isaiah 54:10

Come to Me, all of you who are weary and burdened, and I will give you rest. Matthew 11:28

12

Loss of Appetite

Anticipatory Grief is a complex and profound emotional response to the imminent loss of a loved one or something deeply significant to you. It can leave you feeling overwhelmed, disoriented, and struggling to navigate through your daily life. Often overlooked, one common change that Anticipatory Grief brings is a loss of appetite.

When you experience Anticipatory Grief, your body and mind go through a series of intricate processes that can disrupt your usual eating patterns. This loss of appetite can manifest in different ways, such as a decreased desire to eat, alterations in taste perception, or a general disinterest in food.

The underlying causes of this phenomenon are diverse and may vary from person to person. Emotional factors play a significant role in how Anticipatory Grief affects our appetite. Intense sadness, profound sorrow, and feelings of emptiness can greatly reduce our desire to eat. Your grief can be so overwhelming that it overtakes your ability to focus on basic self-care, including nourishing yourself properly.

Moreover, it triggers a range of physiological responses in your body. Stress hormones, such as cortisol, are released in higher amounts during this period, which can suppress your appetite. These hormones not only affect your hunger levels but can also impact your digestion and metabolism, leading to a feeling of fullness even when you haven't consumed much food. I know this feeling well.

Additionally, Anticipatory Grief often brings about a disruption in your sleep patterns. Sleep disturbances or insomnia can contribute to a loss of appetite, as fatigue and disrupted circadian rhythms can lead to a decreased interest in food.[43]

Effects of appetite changes

If your decreased appetite continues and leads to the onset of malnutrition or deficiencies in vitamins and electrolytes, it is possible for life-threatening complications to arise. As a result, it is of utmost importance to promptly seek medical attention if it persists for a period longer than a few weeks. Ensuring timely medical intervention can be crucial in preventing severe consequences.[44]

A simple way to maintain vitamins in your system is by taking a multivitamin daily and drinking water. If you have lost your taste for water or are normally not a water drinker, try infusing water with fruits and herbs. Infused water does not ordinarily contain sugar but provides a tasty variety to your food plan. Recipes for all types of infused water can be found online. A few different fruits can go a long way in making your own infused water. And it tastes wonderful. I especially love mint, strawberry, orange, and lemon. You might be surprised to find a new favorite flavor.

What to eat when you have no appetite

When you have no appetite, certain foods may be easier to eat and tolerate than others.

Consider these options:

Toast. Whole-grain bread with toppings like avocado or nut butter provides more nutrients and healthy calories compared to plain white toast. It is easily digested and generally well tolerated.

Smoothies. These are easy to consume and can be packed with nutrients and calories in a small portion. Include various fruits or veggies, and add a healthy fat and protein source, like avocado or peanut butter, for added nutrition.

Soups. Keep yourself hydrated with soups that offer a good source of calories from carbohydrates, protein, and fat. Opt for soups that contain vegetables, whole grains, and protein. If you can't finish it all at once, have it in small portions.

Higher-fat yogurt. Yogurt, especially Greek or Icelandic-style, provides protein, minerals, healthy fats, and probiotics. For a nutritious snack, mix plain yogurt with toppings like berries, granola, nuts, or seeds.

Eggs. Nutrient-dense eggs offer essential vitamins and minerals and can be prepared in various ways. Enjoy them however you prefer.[45]

Ultimately, it is better to eat something that sounds appetizing and is well-tolerated rather than skipping meals altogether.

Comfort foods

If you are not inspired by foods you have eaten in the past, you could always make your favorite comfort food. While eating comfort food every day is not the best diet, if it inspires or restarts your appetite, it's definitely worth a try.

Everyone has their own favorite comfort foods, usually created while you were growing up. The memories associated with your favorite comfort foods help to reinforce the comfort in the flavor and texture of the food. Depending on where you grew up, your comfort food could be very different from someone else's. But thanks to the Internet, you have access to recipes of all types.

Some favorite comfort foods include fried chicken, baked potatoes, macaroni and cheese, pizza, spaghetti and meatballs, meatloaf, pancakes, chicken pot pie, apple pie, biscuits and gravy, hamburgers, brownies, and chocolate chip cookies. (The last two are definitely my favorites.) You might have other favorites, but if any of these appeal to you, start there.[46]

Ways to treat loss of appetite

Here are some tips for managing the loss of appetite while experiencing Anticipatory Grief.

If you're struggling to eat, these simple strategies might help.

Set a food alarm. To ensure you don't forget to eat, set a food alarm every 3-4 hours. Even if it's just taking a bite, these reminders can help you maintain a regular eating pattern. If unintentional weight loss becomes a concern, consider incorporating calorie-dense foods like avocados into your meals.

Start with smaller portions. Rather than overwhelming yourself with a full meal, try consuming small amounts of food like snacks or half portions. This can still nourish your body and provide fuel.

Eat at regular intervals. Even if it's just a small portion, try to eat every few hours. This helps establish a routine for your brain to expect food and gradually improve your appetite.

Optimize your biggest meal. Take advantage of the times when you feel the hungriest and consume a nutrient-dense meal or snack. This may be in the morning after the longest period without food or later in the day.

Separate drinks from meals. To ensure a proper balance of nutrients, it's beneficial to save beverages for between meals instead of consuming them with your food. This prevents excessive liquid intake from filling up your stomach.

Incorporate simple exercise if possible. Engaging in exercise over time may help stimulate your appetite. Additionally, certain types of exercise can contribute to muscle growth, which can enhance metabolism and increase your desire to eat.

Keep prepared foods on hand. If the idea of preparing meals overwhelms you, rely on pre-packaged or prepared foods as needed. This ensures that you have access to sustenance without added stress.

Make food more appealing. Adding new colors or flavors to your meals can make them more exciting and enticing, increasing your desire to eat. Maintain a variety of foods with different textures and flavors to satisfy your appetite when it returns.

My Prayer for You

Dear Heavenly Father,

I come before You with a heavy heart, seeking Your comfort and guidance for my dear friend who is coping with Anticipatory Grief and experiencing changes in their appetite. Lord, You are the provider of all needs, and I humbly ask for Your touch upon their physical body during this challenging time.

Father, I acknowledge that Anticipatory Grief can manifest in various ways, and one of those ways is through changes in appetite. I lift this struggle to You, knowing that You are intimately acquainted with every aspect of our bodies and their functions.

Lord, I ask for Your intervention in balancing my friend's appetite. Bring harmony and regulation to their body's hunger signals. Where their appetite feels excessive or insatiable, I pray for Your gentle guidance to eat in moderation and make wise choices that nourish their body. Alternatively, where their appetite is diminished or non-existent, I ask for Your restoration and healing that their body may receive the nourishment it needs.

Father, I pray for Your healing touch upon any physical ailments or discomforts that may be causing changes in appetite. Relieve any pain, digestive issues, or other conditions that may be contributing to their difficulties. Restore their body's natural balance and functions, bringing restoration and health.

Lord, I ask for Your comfort and peace to envelope my dear friend during moments of emotional upheaval, as it can often affect their appetite. Help them find solace in Your love and presence, knowing that You are near to the broken-hearted and can heal and restore. Grant them the strength to find healthy outlets for their emotions and comfort in Your tender embrace.

Father, I pray for wisdom in making food choices that will nourish and support their physical well-being. Guide them in selecting nutritious foods that provide sustenance and strength. Bless them with a balanced and healthy diet that will meet their body's needs and promote overall well-being. Help them to seek professional advice and support if necessary, to ensure they are taking care of their physical health in the most appropriate way.

Lastly, Lord, I lift my dear friend in prayer, asking for Your grace and understanding from those around them. May their loved ones extend empathy, patience, and support during this season of Anticipatory Grief. Help others to recognize the challenges they face with appetite changes and provide the necessary encouragement and care.

Father, I entrust my dear friend and their struggle with appetite changes to Your loving care. Surround them with Your peace and wisdom as they navigate this aspect of Anticipatory Grief. Strengthen their mind, body, and spirit, that they may find balance and healing in Your compassionate embrace.

In the name of Jesus, my Great Healer, I pray, Amen.

Support from The Word

Know that the LORD has set apart the faithful for Himself; the LORD will hear when I call to Him. Psalm 4:3

Listen to my words, Lord; consider my sighing. Pay attention to the sound of my cry, my King and my God, for I pray to You. At daybreak, Lord, You hear my voice; at daybreak I plead my case to You and watch expectantly. Psalm 5:1-3

13 Weakened Immune System | 113

Yet He Himself bore your sicknesses, and He carried your pains; but you in turn regarded Him stricken, struck down by God, and afflicted. But He was pierced because of your transgressions, crushed because of your iniquities; punishment for your peace was on Him, and you are healed by His wounds. Isaiah 53:4-5

But for you who fear My name, the sun of righteousness will rise with healing in its wings, and you will go out and playfully jump like calves from the stall. Malachi 4:2

Heal me, LORD, and I will be healed; save me, and I will be saved, for You are my praise. Matthew 9:35

13
WEAKENED IMMUNE SYSTEM

Anticipatory Grief can make you feel anxious, and this can harm your body. It is important to try and prevent these negative effects. One area of concern is how anxiety affects your immune system. Your immune system is like a shield that protects your body from germs and sickness. It fights off invaders and keeps you healthy. The immune system is powerful and tough, but studies show that too much anxiety, like the kind you feel during Anticipatory Grief, can weaken it. This can also lead to stress in your body, causing the release of cortisol, a hormone linked to stress.

Cortisol, a stress hormone, can lower the immune system. When we are under a lot of stress and worry, cortisol decreases the number of antibodies, thus causing inflammation in an effort to reduce inflammation itself. It also activates natural immunity to address potential problems, but at the same time, it diverts resources away from specific immunities. However, the positive effects of cortisol only work for short periods. If we experience prolonged stress, cortisol keeps on being released, which suppresses the important T-cells and white blood cells needed for a strong immune system. As a result, the immune system gradually weakens over time.

The main worry is not only being more likely to get sick, as exposure to germs is still a factor, but also the body's reduced ability to recover from illness. The cells that are suppressed and attacked are important for fighting off intruders in our body. Stress makes it harder for the immune system to work properly which worsens the recovery process.[47]

Symptoms of a weakened immune system

Take note of these warning signs and discover effective ways to bolster your immune system.

Sky-high stress levels It's not uncommon to notice an increased susceptibility to illness when experiencing Anticipatory Grief or undergoing emotional stress at home. According to the American Psychological Association, long-term stress weakens the responses of the immune system. Nadia Hasan, DO, from Delancey Internal Medicine, explains that stress diminishes the body's lymphocytes, which are white blood cells essential in combating infection. Consequently, lowered lymphocyte levels elevate the risk of viral infections like the common cold.

Persistent cold symptoms Adults typically experience two to three colds per year, with a recovery time of seven to ten days. During this period, the immune system requires three to four days to produce antibodies and combat the invading germs. However, if you frequently catch colds or experience prolonged cold symptoms, it suggests your immune system is struggling to keep pace.

Digestive troubles Frequent occurrences of diarrhea, gas, or constipation can indicate an impaired immune system. Research indicates that nearly 70% of the immune system resides in the digestive tract, where beneficial bacteria and microorganisms defend against infections and support immune function. Insufficient amounts of these beneficial gut bacteria leave you prone to viral infections, chronic inflammation, and even autoimmune disorders.

Slow wound healing After sustaining a burn, cut, or scrape, your skin initiates a healing process by directing nutrient-rich blood to the injury to facilitate new skin growth. This healing process relies on a healthy immune system. However, if your immune system is sluggish, the regeneration of skin becomes difficult, resulting in delayed wound healing.

Recurring infections Frequent battles with infections may indicate underlying issues within your immune system. The American Academy of Allergy, Asthma, & Immunology identifies specific signs of possible immune deficiency in adults, including having four or more ear infections in one year, experiencing pneumonia twice within twelve months, suffering from chronic sinusitis, or enduring more than three episodes of bacterial sinusitis in a year, as well as requiring more than two courses of antibiotics annually.

Chronic fatigue If you consistently feel exhausted despite getting sufficient sleep, it is worth considering whether your immune system is sending you a message. When the immune system struggles, energy levels tend to decline as the body conserves energy to support immune function and combat germs.

Understanding these signs of a weakened immune system empowers you to take proactive measures in strengthening your body's defenses. Implementing lifestyle changes and seeking medical advice when necessary, can significantly enhance your immune system, enabling it to effectively protect you from illnesses.[48]

Improving your immunity

There are several practical ways to enhance your immune system and optimize your overall health. By implementing these strategies, you can reduce the risk of illnesses and maintain a strong immune response:

Eat a nutritious diet. Consuming a well-balanced diet rich in fruits, vegetables, lean proteins, whole grains, and healthy fats can provide essential nutrients for a robust immune system. These nutrients include vitamins A, C, D, E, and zinc, which play a crucial role in maintaining immune function.

Engage in regular physical activity. Staying physically active not only helps manage weight but also strengthens your immune system. Aim for at least 150 minutes of moderate-intensity exercise or 75 minutes of vigorous exercise per week. Choose activities that you enjoy, such as walking, cycling, dancing, or swimming.

Get sufficient sleep. Sleep deprivation can weaken your immune system, making you more susceptible to illnesses. Aim for 7-9 hours of quality sleep each night. Establish a consistent sleep schedule, create a relaxing bedtime routine, and ensure your sleep environment is comfortable and conducive to restful sleep.

Manage stress levels. Chronic stress can hinder your immune system's ability to function effectively. Find healthy ways to manage stress, such as practicing relaxation techniques (deep breathing, yoga, prayer), engaging in hobbies, spending time with loved ones, or seeking professional help when needed.

Maintain a healthy weight. Obesity has been linked to a weakened immune system and increased risk of various health conditions. Incorporate a healthy, balanced diet and regular exercise into your lifestyle to achieve and maintain a healthy weight.

Avoid smoking and limit alcohol consumption. Smoking damages your immune system and increases the risk of respiratory infections. Additionally, excessive alcohol use can weaken your immune system. Quit smoking, and if you consume alcohol, do so in moderation as per current guidelines.

Practice good hygiene. Regularly washing your hands thoroughly with soap and water, or using hand sanitizer when handwashing is not possible, can help prevent the spread of pathogens and reduce the risk of infections. Remember to also cover your mouth and nose with a tissue or your elbow when coughing or sneezing, and avoid close contact with sick individuals to minimize exposure to germs.

Stay up to date with vaccinations. Vaccinations are vital for protecting yourself against various infections and diseases. Keep track of recommended vaccines for your age group and ensure you are up to date.[49]

My Prayer for You

Dear Heavenly Father,

I bow before You, humbled by Your majesty and goodness. I come to You today, with a heart heavy for my precious friend who is grappling with Anticipatory Grief and also facing the challenges of a weakened immune system. I know that You are the ultimate healer and sustainer, and I earnestly seek Your comfort, restoration, and strength for my friend.

Lord, I lift my friend's immune system before You. I recognize the immense toll that Anticipatory Grief can take on the body, leading to a weakened defense against illnesses and infections. I pray that You would infuse their body with renewed strength, healing, and vitality. Strengthen their immune system, Lord, that every cell in their body may be fortified and protected. Restore their health and grant them resilience, oh Lord, that they may experience the fullness of life You have ordained for them.

Father, in Your infinite mercy, envelop my dear friend in Your powerful presence. Surround them with Your loving arms, comforting them in their moments of weakness and distress. Shield them from anxiety, fear, and doubt, and replace it with Your perfect peace that surpasses all understanding.

Lord, I ask for specific guidance and wisdom for my friend to navigate the challenges that a weakened immune system may bring. Grant them discernment to make choices that will enhance their well-being. Help them to prioritize self-care, whether it be through proper nutrition, adequate rest, or any necessary medical interventions. Provide them with a supportive network of healthcare professionals who can assist them along this difficult path.

In the face of uncertainty, grant my friend unshakeable faith. Strengthen their trust in Your divine providence and perfect timing. Remind them that You are their ever-present help, and that even in their weakness, Your strength is made perfect. Renew their hope, dear Lord, as they draw closer to You and find solace in Your steadfast love.

Lord, I also pray for the emotional and spiritual well-being of my dear friend. In the midst of grief and physical struggles, help them to find consolation in Your presence. Grant them moments of joy during sorrow, reminding them of the beauty and blessings that surround them. Comfort them with Your tender mercies and remind them that You are the ultimate healer of hearts.

Lastly, I ask that You bless my friend with a resilient spirit, a heart filled with hope, and an unwavering trust in Your divine plan. May they experience the fullness of Your love and grace, strengthened by the knowledge that You are with them every step of the way.

In the name of Jesus, my Savior, I pray, Amen.

Support from The Word

Be gracious to me, Lord, for I am weak; heal me, Lord, for my bones are shaking; my whole being is shaken with terror. And You, Lord—how long? Turn, Lord! Rescue me; save me because of Your faithful love. Psalm 6:2-4

Turn to me and be gracious to me, for I am alone and afflicted. The distresses of my heart increase; bring me out of my sufferings. Consider my affliction and trouble, and take away all my sins. Psalm 25:16-18

Heal me, Lord, and I will be healed; save me, and I will be saved, for You are my praise. Jeremiah 17:14

Therefore, confess your sins to one another and pray for one another, so that you may be healed. The urgent request of a righteous person is very powerful in its effect. James 5:16

He will wipe away every tear from their eyes. Death will no longer exist; grief, crying, and pain will exist no longer, because the previous things have passed away. Revelation 21:4

14
Pain

One of the most common physical symptoms of Anticipatory Grief is pain. If you are experiencing odd pain right now, you are not alone. Physical pain can manifest in various ways during Anticipatory Grief.

Some common physical pain points include chest pain or tightness, headaches, stomachaches, and typical aches and pains. Pain can also be found in various parts of your body, such as your arms, legs, and hands. And the possibilities are probably greater than these. As everyone experiences Anticipatory Grief differently, your situation will most likely be unique.

The weight of Anticipatory Grief creates an emotional burden that can lead to physical pain. The constant mental anguish, sadness, and overwhelming stress disturb the body's delicate equilibrium, resulting in increased heart rate, elevated blood pressure, and heightened sensitivity to pain. The emotional burden amplifies stress, leading to a state of heightened physical vulnerability.

The pain during Anticipatory Grief not only exacerbates emotional pain but can create a vicious cycle where each reinforces the other. Continuous bodily discomfort and fatigue further compromise emotional resilience, amplifying feelings of sadness, anger, and despair. This spiral creates a reciprocal relationship between physical and emotional pain, making it challenging to find respite from Anticipatory Grief's all-encompassing grip. The inability to find relief or a sense of control over pain can intensify feelings of hopelessness and contribute to declining mental health.[50]

What leads to these physical symptoms? Extensive research demonstrates the profound impact that Anticipatory Grief can have on your body. Anticipatory Grief can escalate inflammation, amplifying existing health issues, such as arthritis, and contributing to the development of new ailments. Your body also releases higher levels of stress hormones that can paralyze the muscles and joints, leading to aches that may persist or fluctuate over a period of weeks to months.[51]

Long-term pain and its side effects

The long-term effects and side effects of pain can lead to challenges in other parts of life. So, closely monitoring your pain level can help in knowing what to do about it. The most common long-term effects and side effects of pain can be managed through self-care. Check out the self-care chapter for more in-depth solutions.

Pain can cause daily life disruption, making it difficult to perform simple tasks or engage in activities you enjoy. Enjoyment is crucial during Anticipatory Grief since it bolsters your emotional, mental, and physical well-being, giving you the strength to deal with daily challenges.

Persistent fatigue caused by pain leads to decreased energy levels and overall diminished quality of life. Fatigue robs you of your favorite activities and even favorite people.

Diminished emotional well-being, a side effect of pain, can lead to feelings of hopelessness and despair. When you have no hope, you have no future.

When you hurt, it's hard to sleep. And when it's hard to sleep, it's difficult to get proper rest. Without proper rest, your thoughts are unclear, and your physical abilities are diminished.

Reduced productivity is also a side effect of pain. Whether you are slowed down by your pain or completely sidelined because of it, your ability to do as much as you used to do is hindered.

If you are in pain and nothing you try seems to ease it, you may have to take sick days. And if you take more sick days than you have accrued, you face the possibility of lost wages.

Even if you can force yourself to go to work in pain, you will still face the challenge of difficulty working. Depending on what you do in your job, whether standing, sitting, or walking, you could still find it difficult to make it through a workday.

Pain can disrupt your cognitive functions, such as memory, attention, and concentration. This mental challenge can lead to stress, which in turn can cause more pain.[52]

How to reduce anticipatory grief pain and muscle tension

During Anticipatory Grief you are already weakened emotionally and mentally. So, when you add pain, it can exacerbate your grief. This cycle can feed on itself and continue to spiral out of control, if left unchecked.

The following list contains ways you can alleviate your pain and end the pain cycle.

Exercise. Exercise is one of the most effective ways to combat stress. This is because it increases the flow of oxygen and nutrients to the muscles, which relaxes them and helps eliminate tension.

Stretch. Stretching can help alleviate muscle pain in addition to increasing flexibility and reducing stress. Yoga and prayer are also great practices to try since they have been linked to lower levels of muscle tension.

Get massages. Messages can help lower tension and promote relaxation, reducing the severity of grief-related pain.

Use hot and cold therapy. Hot and cold therapy is a quick and effective solution for pain relief. A hot bath or shower can reduce stiffness and tension, while ice or a cold compress can reduce inflammation and numb the pain response.

Be in nature. Spend time in nature, since just 20 to 30 minutes of it can lower stress hormone levels by 20%.

Connect. Connecting with others, whether it's in person, by phone, or Internet, as a strong support system helps you become more resilient.[53]

Write. Writing down 3 things you are thankful for each day can redirect your focus from the pain to the good things in your life.

Laugh. Even though you may not think about laughing or even want to laugh right now, it can (and will — I know from personal experience) ease the tension you are experiencing, allowing your body to relax. Check the self-care chapter for a great way to inspire yourself to laugh.

Cry. You may not be a crier, and that's fine. Some people don't cry or even like the idea of crying. But if you can read something or watch something that always touches you deeply, and cry even one or two tears, it could help you feel much better. During my most severe symptoms of Anticipatory Grief, my doctor wrote me a prescription to cry every day, even if it was just one or two tears. And it was amazing how much it helped.

My Prayer for You

Dear Heavenly Father,

I humbly come before You today, seeking Your comfort and strength for my precious friend who is experiencing Anticipatory Grief. I acknowledge that You are the source of all healing, and I trust in Your love and wisdom to guide them through this difficult journey. Lord, I lift to You my dear friend who is burdened with physical pain as they navigate the challenges before them.

Gracious God, I ask that You ease their bodily suffering and grant them relief from the physical anguish they are experiencing. Lord, You have created our bodies fearfully and wonderfully, and You understand the intricacies of our physical beings. I pray that You bring forth Your healing touch, providing comfort, strength, and ease to my friend.

In moments when their body aches, may they find peace in Your presence. Help them to remember that You are their refuge and strength, a very present help in times of trouble. Remind them that You are the Great Physician, and through Your grace, miracles can happen. Fill their hearts with hope, knowing that

You are working all things for their good, even during their physical struggles.

Lord Jesus, You too experienced pain and suffering during Your time on earth. You understand what it means to endure physical affliction. I ask that You draw near to my dear friend in pain, pouring out Your compassion and understanding on them. Comfort them with Your presence and grant them the assurance that they are not alone in their suffering.

Father, I also pray for the loved ones who stand alongside my friend. Grant them wisdom, patience, and strength as they support my friend. Help them to be a source of comfort and encouragement, reminding them of the hope they have in You.

During this season of Anticipatory Grief, Lord, may my friend find solace in Your unfailing love. Guide them in their journey and help them lean on You as their source of strength. Remind them of the eternal hope they have in Jesus, knowing that even during physical pain, there is a glorious and pain-free eternity awaiting those who believe in You.

I offer this prayer in the name of Jesus, my Savior and Healer, Amen.

Support from The Word

Be strong and courageous, all you who put your hope in the LORD. Psalm 31:24

For our hearts rejoice in Him because we trust in His holy name. May Your faithful love rest on us, Yahweh, for we put our hope in You. Psalm 33:21-22

I put my hope in You, Lord; You will answer, Lord my God. Psalm 38:15

"For I know the plans I have for you"—this is the Lord's declaration—"plans for your welfare, not for disaster, to give you a future and a hope. Jeremiah 29:11

... we also rejoice in our afflictions, because you know that affliction produces endurance, endurance produces proven character, and proven character produces hope. This hope will not disappoint us, because God's love has been poured out in your hearts through the Holy Spirit who was given to us. Romans 5:3-5

15
Fatigue

One of the most common physical ailments associated with Anticipatory Grief is fatigue. This is not ordinary fatigue. This is the I-don't-want-to-get-out-of-bed-in-the-morning fatigue. It robs you of interest in things and causes you to neglect people. Your social life dwindles and your motivation is gone. Although you might have been a productive person in the past, you find yourself calling yourself lazy. But don't go there just yet. Although you might feel lazy, you are far from lazy and here's why.

Experiencing fatigue or extreme exhaustion is a typical occurrence during the Anticipatory Grief process. Various factors contribute to this feeling of tiredness, particularly if you are now responsible for the care of your loved one. You are still expected to perform your normal functions, like going to work or taking care of children. But physical, emotional, and cognitive issues can bring on fatigue.

Emotional contributors

Emotional exhaustion due to Anticipatory Grief is an overwhelming experience that drains you mentally, physically, and emotionally. When grieving, you experience a rollercoaster of emotions that can be incredibly draining, leaving you feeling depleted and fatigued.

Sadness is one of the primary emotions experienced during grief, and it can completely consume your energy. The constant weight of sorrow wears on you, leading to a deep-rooted fatigue that is hard to shake off.

Anticipatory Grief often leaves you feeling frustrated and helpless, leading to anger towards the situation or even towards yourself. This pent-up anger adds to the emotional burden, further depleting your energy reserves.

Loneliness is yet another aspect that exacerbates emotional exhaustion during Anticipatory Grief. The anticipated loss of a loved one can leave a void that feels impossible to fill, leading to intense feelings of loneliness and contributing to fatigue, as you struggle to find solace and comfort in your grief-stricken state.[54]

Mental contributors

Mental exhaustion is a common experience during Anticipatory Grief, as it can significantly impact various cognitive processes essential for daily functioning. The cognitive symptoms can manifest as difficulties with concentration, memory, decision-making, and problem-solving.

Difficulties with concentration and memory are prevalent among grieving individuals. Your mind may constantly wander to the impending loss, making it challenging to focus on tasks at hand. You might find yourself forgetting simple things like names, dates, or everyday responsibilities, adding an additional layer of distress.

Decision-making becomes burdensome during Anticipatory Grief. You may struggle to make even the simplest choices, as your cognitive load is already depleted by the grief process. Problem-solving skills can be impaired as well. The ability to see multiple perspectives and generate creative ideas may be compromised, leading to frustration and stress.

These cognitive difficulties contribute to feelings of fatigue. The mental effort required to concentrate, remember, decide, and solve problems drains energy reserves. Grieving individuals often describe feeling mentally and physically exhausted, as these cognitive symptoms demand tremendous cognitive effort and consume a significant portion of their limited emotional energy.[55]

Physical contributors

Physical exhaustion because of the stress of Anticipatory Grief is a common experience, as it can cause a cascade of symptoms that disrupt your normal patterns of sleep, appetite, and overall health.

One of the most significant factors contributing to physical exhaustion during Anticipatory Grief is disrupted sleep patterns. Many people find it difficult to fall asleep or stay asleep, or they may experience frequent nightmares. This continual lack of sleep leaves you feeling mentally and physically drained, contributing to feelings of fatigue.

Another physical symptom commonly experienced during Anticipatory Grief is a loss of appetite. The decreased intake of nutrients and energy further contributes to physical exhaustion.

Furthermore, Anticipatory Grief has been found to weaken the immune system. The chronic stress of grief activates the release of cortisol, a hormone that suppresses the immune system's response to infections and diseases. This weakened immune system makes individuals more susceptible to illnesses, frequent infections, and prolonged recovery periods.[56]

Ways to combat fatigue

Prioritize self-care. Focus on taking care of your physical and emotional needs. Make sure you are getting enough sleep, eating well, and engaging in activities that bring you joy and relaxation.

Seek support. Reach out to loved ones, friends, or support groups that can provide emotional support. Sharing your feelings and experiences with others who understand can be comforting and help alleviate some of the fatigue.

Establish a routine. Creating a structured daily routine can help provide a sense of stability and predictability, which can be soothing during times of grief. Ensure your routine includes rest periods and activities that recharge you.

Practice relaxation techniques. Engage in activities that promote relaxation, such as deep breathing exercises, prayer, yoga, or listening to calming music. These practices can help reduce stress and alleviate fatigue.

Exercise regularly. Engaging in regular physical activity, even if it's gentle exercise like going for a walk, can improve your energy levels and boost your mood. Regular exercise also helps promote better sleep.

Allow yourself to grieve. Give yourself permission to feel and express your emotions. Suppressing grief can lead to emotional exhaustion. Allow yourself time to process your feelings, whether through journaling, talking with someone, or engaging in other therapeutic activities.

Set realistic expectations. Recognize that grief-induced fatigue is normal and be kind to yourself. You may not have the same energy levels as before; so, adjust your expectations and give yourself grace as you navigate this difficult time.

Take breaks and rest. Allow yourself breaks throughout the day to rest and recharge. Listen to your body and give yourself the rest you need without feeling guilty or forcing yourself to keep going.

Engage in activities that bring comfort. Find activities that provide comfort and solace, such as reading, listening to music, spending time in nature, or engaging in creative pursuits. These activities can help reduce fatigue by providing emotional nourishment.

Consider seeking professional help. If your Anticipatory Grief-induced fatigue becomes overwhelming or persists for an extended period, consider reaching out to a mental health professional who can provide guidance and support in dealing with your grief. They can help you develop coping strategies specific to your situation and provide a safe space for you to process your emotions.[57][58]

My Prayer for You

Dear Heavenly Father,

During Anticipatory Grief, I come before You with a heavy heart, seeking Your comfort and peace. Today, I specifically lift my precious friend who is grappling with the burdensome weight of physical fatigue. Lord, You are the source of our strength, and I know that You deeply understand the weariness they feel.

Loving God, I ask that You intervene in their life and provide them with renewed energy and endurance. I humbly request that You alleviate the physical fatigue they are experiencing, as their body bears the weight of their grief and sorrow. Restore their strength, Lord, and grant them moments of respite from the weariness that engulfs them.

You, O Lord, are the everlasting God, the Creator of the ends of the earth. You never grow tired or weary, and You promise to strengthen those who wait upon You. I claim Your promise today, Lord, and ask that You infuse my dear friend with Your divine power and vitality.

Holy Spirit, pour out Your refreshing presence upon their tired soul. Grant them moments of rest and restoration, enabling them to find peace during their weariness. As they lean on You, may they experience an inner transformation, shifting their focus from their own strength to Your all-sufficient grace.

Father, be their comfort and refuge when exhaustion overwhelms them. Remind them that they do not face these challenges alone, for You are with them every step of the way.

Surround them with Your loving arms and provide comfort and peace that surpasses all understanding.

Lord Jesus, You carried the weight of the world on Your shoulders. You understand what it means to be physically fatigued and drained. Through Your own suffering, You empathize with their struggles. I ask that You draw near to my friend, whispering words of comfort and strength and placing Your healing touch upon their weary bodies.

In their weakest moments, help them to find solace in Your promise that Your grace is sufficient. Remind them that Your power is made perfect in weakness. As they surrender their fatigue to You, may they discover a peace that surpasses all understanding.

I offer this prayer in the name of Jesus, my Comforter and Restorer, Amen.

Support from The Word

The Lord is my shepherd; there is nothing I lack. He lets me lie down in green pastures; He leads me beside quiet waters. Psalm 23:1-2

But as for me—poor and in pain— let Your salvation protect me, God. Psalm 69:29

You will keep the mind that is dependent on You in perfect peace, for it is trusting in You. Isaiah 26:3

For I satisfy the thirsty person and feed all those who are weak. Jeremiah 31:25

Come to Me, all of you who are weary and burdened, and I will give you rest. All of you, take up My yoke and learn from Me, because I am gentle and humble in heart, and you will find rest for yourselves. For My yoke is easy and My burden is light. Matthew 11:28-30

Part 4
Relational Challenges

> In anticipatory grief, you're caught between holding on and letting go. You want to make the most of the time you have left, but inwardly prepare yourself for the inevitable goodbye. – Cindi Dawson

My mother was a woman of varied talents. From the time I was born until I got married, she sewed all my clothes and my sisters' clothes—dresses, "play clothes," and even my wedding and bridesmaids' dresses. When I received a new doll at Christmas, she would even make new clothes for the doll. I didn't inherit that gift, though two of my sisters did. Instead, I learned a different valuable lesson. She demonstrated her love and care for others by doing.

When you are experiencing the extreme darkness of the Anticipatory Grief tunnel, it can be easy to withdraw from your routine and become a hermit. I know this from my own experiences. But instead of indulging in sorrow, I found it much easier and more fulfilling to turn my focus on others, particularly my loved one, and help them through their own grief. That doesn't mean you have to deny your feelings. It only means that when you care about others' needs, it enables you to handle your own challenges better.

Growing up in rural Alabama, my mother learned to cook and bake at a very young age. Our Christmas and Easter family dinners were highlighted by her homemade rolls. She loved baking and made cookies, cakes, pies, and cobblers. But more than making these delicious desserts, she loved sharing them with homebound, hospitalized, and hurting friends and neighbors. I remember creamy mints, Texas sheath cakes (my personal favorite), and triple layered sandwiches cut in small triangles for my wedding reception. She was always giving to us and to others.

If you have a skill or ability, could you share it with your loved one and their family? If so, you could be a blessing to them when they truly need it. Think about your talents and how you could use them to help your loved one. Using your skills for others blesses you as well. Helping your loved one could be the light you need to navigate the Anticipatory Grief tunnel.

Another skill my mother possessed was gardening. Every spring she would sit down with my dad to plan out what she wanted to grow along with how many rows she would need of each vegetable. Daddy's contribution was tilling the garden for her. But she did something I didn't understand for a long time. Between every second or third row of veggies, she planted a row or two of flowers. This was such a mystery I finally asked her why. The answer was simple. She grew the flowers to share. She filled vases with bouquets as gifts for others as well as for our house. Yet again she was demonstrating love for others.

I have always remembered this lesson. During my seasons of Anticipatory Grief, I shared with my family and friends. Toward the end of my mother's life, she was in a memory care facility. My older sister and I visited her every day. When it was time to leave, we hugged her, kissed her on the cheek, and told her how much we loved her. One evening when we were saying goodbye, another woman resident meekly asked, "Can I have a hug?" It broke my heart. I thought of my mother's giving spirit; so, I leaned down, hugged her, kissed her on the cheek, and said, "I love you." The smile on her face was so bright and beautiful that when I think of it now, it brings tears to my eyes. What you give and share with others says so much more than you can ever know. And blessing that woman blessed me beyond words can say. Use your gifts—make a quilt, take some flowers, bake some brownies. Give a hug and a kiss on the cheek and say, "I love you." Your heart will rejoice and your trip through the tunnel will be brighter.

16
What to Say

Dealing with a loved one's chronic or terminal illness is an emotional journey that can evoke a myriad of complicated feelings. It is a time when communication becomes more critical than ever; yet finding the right words to say can feel incredibly challenging. If you are your loved one's caregiver, you may have more things to talk about than those included in this chapter. During these difficult moments, it is essential to offer support, empathy, and understanding to your loved one.

The emotions described in Section 1 are challenging to live with every day, but seeing and interacting with your loved one is much more challenging. Your loved one is in front of you, and you can see their emotions, pain, and anxiety as they face their future. It's important to prepare yourself before seeing them for the first or subsequent times.

Set a time to get together. If your loved one is able, getting together on a regular basis could be very beneficial and encouraging to both of you. The first get-together, whether in person, over the phone, or online, depending on your geographic location, can set the tone for future conversations.

The following guidelines are included to help you know what to say and how to say it. I created these guidelines as I journeyed through the Anticipatory Grief tunnel, adding and deleting what worked and did not work through the process.

Create a safe and non-judgmental space. Creating this space for open and honest communication can provide immense relief for both of you. Encouraging your loved one to share any concerns, regrets, or unresolved matters can help alleviate the burden they may be carrying. By expressing a genuine interest in listening to their thoughts and emotions, you can empower your loved one to express their concerns. Assure them that their feelings are valid and that you are there to support them through this difficult time. By encouraging these conversations, you can offer them the opportunity to seek closure, make amends, or simply express themselves freely.

Use active Listening. Incorporating active listening and validating your loved one's experiences is crucial during conversations with them. Practice active listening by giving them your undivided attention, making eye contact, and providing verbal and non-verbal cues that you are truly present and engaged in their words. Responding with empathy and compassion can further validate their experiences and emotions. Let them know that their feelings are completely valid and understandable. By doing so, you create a space of acceptance and understanding that can promote healing and bring them a sense of comfort and reassurance. Remember, the power of active listening and validation lies not only in the spoken words, but also in the caring and compassionate presence you bring to the conversation.

Memories are important. Share favorite memories that bring laughter and warmth. Recall funny moments that you both experienced together. These memories can provide a sense of joy and bring a smile to their face, even in their current state. Remind them of cherished times you spent together. These shared memories can strengthen your bond and create a sense of comfort and companionship.

Honor their interests. If they enjoy crafting, offer to spend an afternoon creating a memorable project. If they are fond of music, listen to their favorite songs together, play a musical instrument, or sing to them or sing together. Engaging in these activities not only provides opportunities for shared moments of joy but also creates an atmosphere of relaxation and happiness. Always remember to be patient and compassionate, understanding that their illness may limit their abilities, and adapt activities accordingly to ensure their comfort and enjoyment.

While enduring Anticipatory Grief with Mark, my business partner, he was unable to speak due to a permanent trach. So, we strategized about the business with me asking questions out loud and him writing the answers on paper. We shared a common interest in music, him playing the trumpet and me being a singer. I sang to him on several occasions although it made me feel guilty at times because it made him cry. But he always appreciated my singing, demonstrating his feelings by squeezing my hand. If you are unsure about what to do, feel free to ask. By the way, I saved every piece of paper he used to answer my questions and ask me for help, and they still hold a special place in my heart and office.

Lend spiritual support. If you and your loved one share spiritual beliefs, you can create some spiritual memories while navigating the Anticipatory Grief tunnel together. Praying and reading the Bible can encourage your loved one and support your common challenges. You can share some specific prayer concerns before praying. Either you can pray by yourself, if you feel comfortable doing that, or you both can pray aloud. You can also ask what their favorite scripture passages are, make a note of them, and volunteer to read them aloud for comfort. You can also ask, "What can I say or do right now that will help you?" If they don't answer, just let them know you are with them and then sit quietly.

My dad was a bi-vocational pastor, working as an engineer fulltime during the week and pastoring on weekends. I can't remember a time when he did not pray with people in their homes or in the hospital. He would occasionally take our whole family with him to visit someone who was sick. It was a valuable and much-appreciated example that still serves me well today. My sisters and I sang together growing up, and we shared our love for music during hospital visits, sometimes singing the patient's favorite hymn. So, I know firsthand how much spiritual comfort can help.

Be prepared for difficult situations The stress of Anticipatory Grief can be overwhelming, and you can't prepare for every possibility. You might want to be prepared for unexpected emotional and physical outbursts like crying, anger, or cursing. Your loved one is facing an unplanned and unpredictable future, and the "not knowing" part of their future can produce atypical reactions. I have witnessed name calling, blaming, throwing things, refusal to eat or drink, uncontrolled crying, and more. But if you are prepared for the unplanned, and know that unusual behavior could happen, you will be able to handle it more calmly. Remaining compassionate and encouraging can go a long way.

Examples of what to say

The following examples are included to help you know what to say when you speak with your loved one. Pick one that feels comfortable and sounds like what you would say, or modify it slightly to feel more like you. If you are concerned about whether you will look and sound authentic, practice saying it in front of a mirror several times. When the situation calls for it, feel free to use it.

"I am so sorry."

"You are in my heart."

"I'm praying for you and your family."

"Would you like me to email you funny or sweet videos on a regular basis?"

"I hate that you're going through this."

"We / I miss you."

"Can I come over this weekend?" Or "can I come over next Tuesday afternoon?" Don't ask your loved one to be the social secretary. Specify a time and BE THERE!

"I love you."

"May I add you to my church's prayer list?"

"You inspire me."

"I'm here and available for you."

"Thank you for letting me know" (after they have given you the initial news). "Can we pray right now?"

"Here's my phone number."
"I want to spend time with you."

Examples of what NOT to say

If you don't know what to say and the list of options above doesn't resonate with you, you may be tempted to say something like the following phrases. DON'T DO IT! If you truly care for this person, saying something like the following statements can alienate your loved one and damage your relationship. If you just can't bring yourself to say something, then don't say anything. It's all right to remain silent but refrain from saying any of the following statements.

"You'll be all right."
"Everything will work out all right."
"It's not as bad as it seems."
"Things will get better."
"I know how you feel."
"I've been through this with my (insert relationship here), and they got better."
"Your situation reminds me of the time that I …"
"You'll beat this."
"I'll check in with you periodically to see what you need."

If you want to help, see the following chapter on how to help. You will find some things you can do and when to do them.

My Prayer for You

Gracious and loving Father,

Today, I come before You burdened for my precious friend who is experiencing Anticipatory Grief and facing the challenge of knowing what to say to their loved one. I acknowledge that navigating conversations during such a difficult time can be overwhelming and emotionally complex. I seek Your guidance and wisdom, Lord, as they navigate these relational waters.

Father, I ask that You grant them the right words to express their love, care, and support. Give them discernment and sensitivity to understand the needs and desires of their loved one. Help them to be vessels of comfort, providing a safe space for open and honest communication.

Lord, I pray that You fill my dear friend's heart with compassion, empathy, and understanding. Help them to truly listen, not only to the words being spoken but also to the unspoken emotions hidden in their loved one's heart. May they be able to acknowledge the pain and struggles their loved one is experiencing, and to understand those emotions with love and care.

Father, I recognize that everyone copes with grief differently, and each person's needs vary. Grant them the wisdom to discern what their loved one needs—whether it be a listening ear, a comforting presence, a shared memory, or simply a tender touch. May they convey their love and support through their actions and words, offering kindness, reassurance, and understanding.

Lord Jesus, You are the Great Comforter and the Prince of Peace. I invite You to be present in these conversations. Fill every interaction with Your divine love and grace, providing a sense of peace and comfort that surpasses all understanding. Give them the words that will bring comfort, hope, and encouragement to their loved one during this challenging season.

Holy Spirit, be their guide and counselor. Help them to rely on Your divine wisdom and guidance as they interact with their loved one. Grant them the courage to ask questions, to actively listen, and to offer prayers of comfort and healing. May Your presence be a source of strength and comfort, reminding them that they are never alone in these conversations.

Father, I also pray for their loved one. Surround them with Your love and peace, and may Your presence bring them comfort and assurance. Grant them moments of deep connection with their family and friends, allowing them to share their hearts and find solace in the love that surrounds them.

I offer this prayer in the precious name of Jesus, my ever-present Helper, Amen.

Support from The Word

The LORD is good, a stronghold in a day of distress; He cares for those who take refuge in Him. Nahum 1:7

"Your heart must not be troubled. Believe in God; believe also in Me. In My Father's house are many dwelling places; if not, I would have told you. I am going away to prepare a place for you. If I go away and prepare a place for you, I will come back and receive you to Myself, so that where I am you may be also. You know the way to where I am going." John 14:1-4

"Peace I leave with you. My peace I give to you. I do not give to you as the world gives. Your heart must not be troubled or fearful." John 14:27

Now may the God of hope fill you with all joy and peace as you believe in Him so that you may overflow with hope by the power of the Holy Spirit. Romans 15:13

Praise the God and Father of your Lord Jesus Christ, the Father of mercies and the God of all comfort. He comforts you in all your affliction, so that you may be able to comfort those who are in any kind of affliction, through the comfort you yourselves receive from God. For as the sufferings of Christ overflow to us, so through Christ your comfort also overflows. 2 Corinthians 1:3-5

17
How to Help your Loved One

While you are navigating the Anticipatory Grief tunnel, it can be easy to forget about your loved one's needs. It isn't that you don't care about them because, of course, you do. But knowing what to do to help can be daunting. In this chapter you will discover many ways that you can be of help. As you read, make a list of the ones you want to implement and add ideas that come to mind as you read.

Provide emotional support. Chronic or terminal illnesses can bring on a range of emotions for your loved one. The first and most crucial thing you can do is to offer unwavering emotional support. Be patient, understanding, and empathetic. Encourage them to express their feelings and concerns, and simply be there to listen.

Be a source of comfort. Physical touch can have a profound impact on someone facing illness. Offer comforting gestures such as giving gentle hugs, holding their hand, or offering a reassuring presence. Sometimes, silence and a comforting touch can provide more solace than words.

Accompany them to appointments. Medical appointments and treatments can be overwhelming and stressful. Offer to accompany your loved one to these appointments, providing both emotional support and an extra set of ears. Take notes, ask questions, and be their advocate to ensure they receive the best possible care.

Be an advocate. Navigating the healthcare system can be complex, especially for those facing chronic or terminal illnesses. Help your loved one understand their options, assist in filling out paperwork, and be their advocate when communicating with doctors and healthcare professionals. Ensure their voice is heard and their concerns are addressed.

Assist with daily tasks. Offer to help with household chores like cleaning, cooking, laundry, or running errands. Accomplishing these tasks can provide much-needed relief and allow your loved one to focus on their health. Feed their pets if they have any, walk their dog, clean out the litter box, and support their furry friends. Fur angels can provide much-needed support.

Offer transportation. Medical appointments, treatments, and therapies may require regular transportation. Providing rides to and from these appointments can significantly ease the burden on your loved one. Coordinate schedules and be reliable to ensure they reach their destinations comfortably and on time.

Offer respite for caregivers. If your loved one has a caregiver, recognize that they too need time to recharge. Offer to take over caregiving duties for a few hours or even a day, allowing the primary caregiver to rest and rejuvenate. This gesture can provide them with much-needed relief and reduce burnout.

Assist with medical needs. Offer to help your loved one manage their medications by organizing pill boxes, keeping track of prescription refills, or even administering medication if needed. Ensure they understand their treatment plan and any potential side effects.

Share hobbies or interests. Engaging in activities your loved one enjoys can provide a welcome distraction and offer moments of joy. Spend quality time with them by reading together, watching movies, playing games, or engaging in hobbies they love. These shared experiences can provide a sense of normalcy and strengthen bonds.

Bring them favorite foods or treats. Food can comfort and uplift spirits. Prepare or bring your loved one their favorite meals, snacks, or desserts. Take into consideration any dietary restrictions or preferences they may have. A special treat can brighten their day and show your thoughtfulness and care. If you know their favorite eateries, arrange in advance to bring them a meal or snack from those favorite places.

Engage in gentle exercises. Depending on their health condition, your loved one may benefit from light exercise or movement. Help them with gentle exercises like stretching, walking, or yoga as appropriate. Physical activity can improve their overall well-being and contribute to maintaining strength and mobility. If their strength is low, arrange to take them outdoors to enjoy the sun and breeze.

Help with technical needs. In today's digital age, technology plays a significant role in staying connected. Assist your loved one in setting up electronic devices, teaching them to use video call platforms, or managing online activities. This support can help them stay connected with friends, family, and support groups, or even access telehealth services.

Provide entertainment. During challenging times, distractions and entertainment can be important for mental well-being. Bring books, magazines, puzzles, or other hobbies your loved one can enjoy during their downtime. These activities can provide a welcome escape and offer a sense of normalcy. While my sister was receiving infusions, we would take a game we could play together as a group. It was so much fun that even other patients having infusions and their caregivers joined the game.

Offer companionship. Loneliness is often an unwelcome companion for those facing chronic or terminal illnesses. Spend quality time with your loved one, engaging in conversation, sharing stories, or simply being present. Your companionship can make a significant difference in their emotional well-being and help them feel connected and loved. It can also help your own loneliness if you are experiencing it as well.

Support their family. Chronic or terminal illnesses affect not only the individual but also their immediate family members. Offer support and a listening ear to their family members who may also be facing challenges in their caregiving roles. Offer assistance, when possible, whether it's running errands, providing transportation, or simply being there for them to talk to.

Use old-school handwritten notes. In this age of technology, it's often easy to forget what a written note or card can do. Receiving something in the mail can put a smile on your loved one's face even when you are not there with them. Whether it's a card or a note, it shows that you are thinking about them. Consider enclosing a small gift card occasionally just to add another layer of surprise.

Call and volunteer. Another one of those personal touches often forgotten in this technology-based world is the phone call. Why not call your loved one and talk for a few minutes? Remember to be respectful of their energy level. While you are chatting, offer, "I'm heading to the grocery store. What can I get for you?" and bring it to them. Or "I'm heading to the gas station and then I'm going to get my car washed. Can I come by and get your car to do the same for you?" Remember to ask specific, open-ended questions, not questions that can be answered with a simple "yes" or "no." You will get a much more honest answer. And you can be helpful.

Helping your loved one goes beyond simply being present. By providing practical assistance and emotional support, and acting as an advocate, you can make an enormous difference in their journey. From accompanying them to appointments to engaging in shared activities, your support can bring comfort, strength, and moments of joy during their challenging times. Remember, your presence and care can make all the difference in their lives.

My Prayer for You

Dear Heavenly Father,

I come before You today with a heavy heart, seeking Your comfort and guidance for my friend who is facing Anticipatory Grief as they walk alongside their loved one. I lift to You the deep and complex emotions they experience as they grapple with how to best support and help their loved one in this difficult time. I seek Your wisdom and understanding, Lord, to navigate the relational challenges they encounter.

Compassionate God, I ask that You grant my friend the strength and courage to be a source of comfort and support. Help them to approach their loved one with sensitivity and empathy, understanding that each person's needs and desires may differ. Grant them the ability to listen deeply, to enter into their loved one's perspective, and to respond with genuine compassion.

Lord, in their interactions and conversations, give them the right words and actions to demonstrate their love, care, and support. May they be a source of comfort and stability during moments of distress or pain. Help them to create a safe space where their loved one can freely express their emotions, fears, and hopes. Grant them patience, understanding, and the ability to validate their loved one's emotions, even when they may struggle to understand or relate fully.

Father, I pray that if they find themselves in a caregiver role, they will have divine discernment and wisdom as they navigate the medical challenges their loved one faces. Give them clarity in understanding treatment options, decision-making processes, and ways to alleviate their loved one's suffering. May they be a trusted advocate and partner in the healthcare journey, working together with medical professionals to ensure the highest quality of care and comfort.

Lord Jesus, You are the ultimate example of love and compassion. Teach them to follow Your example in their relationship with their loved one. May they seek to serve and selflessly care for them, putting their own emotions aside temporarily for the sake of their loved one's well-being. Fill them with grace and strength to offer gentle words, acts of kindness, and supportive gestures that communicate their love and devotion.

Holy Spirit, be their guide and source of comfort as they face these challenging times. Grant them wisdom, strength, and peace in their role as a supportive presence. May they lean on You for guidance, knowing that You understand their pain and are with them every step of the way.

Father, I also pray for their loved one. Surround them with Your love and peace, providing them comfort and assurance in the midst of their challenges. Give them moments of joy, strength, and deep connection with their family and friends. May their relationships be filled with grace, forgiveness, and reconciliation in these final days.

I offer this prayer in the powerful name of Jesus, my Comforter and Healer, Amen.

Support from The Word

But He said to me, "My grace is sufficient for you, for My power is perfected in weakness." Therefore, I will most gladly boast all the more about my weaknesses, so that Christ's power may reside in me. So, I take pleasure in weaknesses, insults, catastrophes, persecutions, and in pressures, because of Christ. For when I am weak, then I am strong. 2 Corinthians 12:9-10

Don't worry about anything, but in everything, through prayer and petition with thanksgiving, let your requests be made known to God. Philippians 4:6

Therefore, you may boldly say, "The Lord is my helper; I will not be afraid. What can man do to me?" Hebrews 13:6

Humble yourselves, therefore, under the mighty hand of God, so that He may exalt you at the proper time, casting all your care on Him, because He cares about you. 1 Peter 5:6-7

He will wipe away every tear from their eyes. Death will no longer exist; grief, crying, and pain will exist no longer, because the previous things have passed away. Revelation 21:4

18
Familial Anticipatory Grief

Familial Anticipatory Grief is a term I started using while witnessing the gradual decline of my mother's memory due to vascular dementia. I never said it out loud or talked about it; I just noticed it and then paid closer attention to it. I used it to refer to the collective grief that we all went through as we watched her fade away. We each experienced our own individual grief while we still needed to navigate the collective grief within our family. It's a tricky and very tight curve in the Anticipatory Grief tunnel, but it can happen to you, whether it's your family, work, club, or church. So, it is worth analyzing and understanding.

At the risk of stating the obvious, everyone is different. And everyone's personality is different. In a group setting where people interact with each other regularly, personalities sometimes clash. During the highly emotional time of Anticipatory Grief, the group dynamics can be even trickier to navigate. The permutations of emotional responses at different times can be too great to calculate. So, how do you handle all this emotion from so many people at the same time? That is a great question.

The goal of this chapter is to provide some practical ways to deal with Familial Anticipatory Grief. While I use the term "familial," apply this chapter to your particular group setting. Whether you are close to your loved one or a bystander, the emotional depth of the grieving family can take a toll on you. Let's look at some ways you can navigate your own emotions while interacting with others navigating theirs.

Be aware of time. The first and biggest thing I noticed was time and how it affected our family. Accepting our new reality took time, especially since we never expected it. Time is one of the greatest gifts we have, and it can serve us well if we give it the credit it deserves. Don't try to make sense of what is happening in one sitting. Give yourself time to breathe, take it in, adapt to your new normal, and feel better. When you can breathe, try to understand the diagnosis, educate yourself, and then take it one day at a time. Every night that you sleep will be another day past the initial news.

Be mindful of your family's coping style. Families have different ways of dealing with crises and their feelings. Some families discuss their emotions openly, while others tend to deal with their problems privately. The emotions and coping skills of a club, church, or office might be guided by its leadership, so interactions might be controlled, leaving you to handle your emotions alone. But a family may be more varied and vocal in their emotions. Your experience as a family member will guide you in recognizing the normal behavioral and emotional patterns of your family. Be mindful of your family's coping style and, if possible, help them communicate better.

Adjust to changing family roles. A family member's lack of participation due to illness will change roles, routines, responsibilities, and activities. You might be called on to assume responsibilities you don't feel prepared to handle. But your willingness to "pitch in and do your part" will help other family members recognize your support. Your previous responsibilities might be handed to someone else who is capable, so you are called on to guide them in their new responsibilities. The time of day or day of the week that you perform certain chores might change, disrupting your normal routine. These seemingly small changes can add to the overall upheaval of the family unit. It's essential to support and empathize with each other during this time and adjust to the new situation.

Consider getting outside help. If someone in your family is the primary caregiver for your loved one, it could prove very beneficial to look outside of the family for help. Look for grocery delivery, yard maintenance, housekeeping, or transportation services. If you face Anticipatory Grief at work, maybe you could use a temporary or remote contractor to fill in. For a club or church group, dividing the responsibilities among 3 or 4 other people could ease the burden of assuming too many new roles.

Understand and respect your loved one's emotions. People with chronic or terminal illnesses go through different emotions. Fear, anxiety, anger, guilt, sadness, and loneliness are just a few of the emotions they may feel. Let them express their thoughts and feelings freely without trying to change them. Listen, understand, and offer support, but don't judge. Let them say what they need to say without making them feel uncomfortable. If something your loved one shares hurts your feelings or scares you, try to remain calm. They are coping with even more than you are. If talking to everyone in the family at once is too exhausting for your loved one, limit your time together to one or two people at a time.

Create a support group within your family. Meet together on a regular basis. While work, school, and extracurricular schedules are hard to juggle, it is worth it to stay connected and on task. Showing support for all members of your family is key when facing such a challenging time together. Meeting on a regular basis – weekly or bi-weekly – to discuss how you are coping is crucial.

Be helpful to your family members. When emotions are high and you are given new responsibilities, you can constantly feel on edge. So, make the secondary focus of your family meetings an opportunity to help. Be willing to offer encouragement to others. Ask how you can help with ways to manage their physical, emotional, mental, and spiritual needs. Be honest and ask when you need support in these areas as well. During your family meeting, rather than finding fault with other family members, find something to thank someone for since your last meeting. Be vocally positive and build your relationships.

Help your family members care for themselves. Don't lose sight of self-care during this difficult time. Encourage everyone to take care of themselves by getting enough rest, eating balanced meals, and planning fun events. When you are going through a stressful time, like Anticipatory Grief, you need to do something specific and special just for yourself every day. That means Every. Single. Day. Even though you might have more to do than you think can be done in 24 hours, realize that self-care is very important, especially now. So, to strengthen your emotional well-being, make sure you enjoy your own special thing every day. Then encourage your family members to identify theirs and do it every day as well.

Acknowledge that every family member, including you, is not themselves right now. Just knowing that can help you understand why they might act the way they do. And if there are any strained relationships or unresolved conflicts between family members, they can be magnified right now. I know about family conflicts. I've been there, done that myself. So, I understand that this might be very challenging to work through. To the best of your ability, try to resolve or set aside disagreements and past hurts for the time being to get through this painful journey together. If possible, instead of remembering the past and what led to your current rift, focus on maintaining a peaceful atmosphere within your home and between you and your family members to ease your stress.

Lean on your spirituality. If faith is part of your family's life, express it in ways you find appropriate. Attend church, read the Bible, or pray together. Allow yourselves the time to be around people who understand and support your religious beliefs. Small groups are the best for this. My Sunday School class, all women, was my greatest support group during my experiences with Anticipatory Grief. I can't stress this enough. If your spiritual beliefs are strong and you feel comfortable doing so, you could close your family meetings in prayer, asking for help for yourself and each other.

Seek hope and healing together. Every family member will grieve differently, so leave room for different expressions of grief. Reconciling your Anticipatory Grief will take time, so love and support each other while being kind to yourselves.

My Prayer for You

Loving Heavenly Father,

I come before You today, burdened by Anticipatory Grief and seeking Your love and guidance in the midst of this difficult journey. I lift to You my precious friend who is coping with the challenges of Anticipatory Grief within their family unit. I ask for Your presence and wisdom as they navigate this season together, supporting and loving one another.

Gracious God, I pray for unity within the family during this time of grief. Help them to come together, knowing that they are stronger when they face these challenges as a united front. Bind their hearts together with cords of love, understanding, and compassion. May they be a source of strength and comfort for one another, recognizing that they are on this journey together.

Lord, I ask for Your healing touch upon any strained relationships within the family unit. Mend any brokenness, soothe any conflicts, and restore a spirit of harmony and peace. Help them to set aside their differences and focus on the common goal of supporting and uplifting one another through this difficult time. Fill their hearts with empathy, grace, and forgiveness, allowing love to reign over all interactions.

Father, I pray for open communication within the family. Grant them the courage to express their fears, concerns, and emotions honestly and authentically. Help them to listen with patience and understanding, providing a safe space for each family member to share their thoughts and feelings without judgment. Give them wisdom to offer words of comfort and encouragement, and help them to truly hear and understand one another.

Lord Jesus, You experienced grief and loss during Your time on earth, and You understand the complexities of familial relationships. Draw near to this family and fill them with Your love and compassion. Pour out Your healing and comforting presence upon them, so that they may find solace in Your embrace.

Holy Spirit, be the source of strength and peace within each family member's heart. Grant them the courage to support one another, even when faced with their own grief and struggles. Guide them in embracing compassion and empathy as they walk alongside each other, offering a listening ear, a comforting shoulder, and a touch of love.

Father, I also pray for moments of joy and gratitude amidst the pain of Anticipatory Grief. Help them to find and savor the precious memories and moments they have together as a family. Nourish their spirits with hope and remind them that life is a gift, even in the face of grief.

I offer this prayer in the name of Jesus, my Comforter and Redeemer, Amen.

Support from The Word

The LORD is a refuge for the oppressed, a refuge in times of trouble. Those who know Your name trust in You because You have not abandoned those who seek You, Yahweh. Psalm 9:9-10

The LORD is my rock, my fortress, and my deliverer, my God, my mountain where I seek refuge, my shield and the horn of my salvation, my stronghold. Psalm 18:2

The eyes of the LORD are on the righteous, and His ears are open to their cry for help. Psalm 34:15

I am afflicted and needy; the Lord thinks of me. You are my helper and my deliverer; my God, do not delay. Psalm 40:17

"For I know the plans I have for you" – this is the Lord's declaration – "plans for your welfare, not for disaster, to give you a future and a hope." Jeremiah 29:11

19
The Unofficial Rules of Anticipatory Grief

It sounds so simple. Just start each day with a positive attitude. Pray, read the Bible, and lean on your Sunday School class for support and you'll be fine. But that dream is far from a reality. The dream doesn't consider your emotions, thoughts, health, relationships, and spiritual well-being. Wouldn't it be great if the dream was a reality? But life isn't a dream, contrary to song lyrics.

This chapter focuses on the dos and don'ts of Anticipatory Grief. These are not written in stone, so don't feel overwhelmed thinking there's no way you can follow them. The rules are only guideposts for what you might experience during this challenging season of your life. They are presented so you don't wake up one morning and say, "Why did THAT happen?" "Why do I feel like THIS?" "Why didn't I do THAT?"

I compiled these "rules" through several journeys of Anticipatory Grief. Some of them came to me after months, and some were instant flashes of clarity. But I included them because many of them were things I wish I had known before going through the tunnel or while meandering through the twists and turns of the Anticipatory Grief tunnel. Some will apply to you, but not all will. When something doesn't apply to you, feel free to return to it later and focus on the ones that do speak to your situation right now.

Dealing with a returning illness

Dealing with "on again, off again" sickness can be an unprecedented roller coaster of emotions. The most common demonstration of this situation is cancer that has been treated but returns months or even years later. You have already witnessed your loved one's journey through treatment and recovery or remission, and you probably felt much better when you got the "all clear" diagnosis. So, you gradually relax and begin to live a "normal" life again.

When you get the news, "It's back," you may be angry and say, "This was all settled. It's not fair! It can't be true!" But bravely you think you'll be prepared and able to handle it. Sadly, that is not always the case. Be prepared for it to be a totally different experience this time. Your emotions, health, relationships, and spiritual well-being might not follow the same patterns they did before. Depending on how you look at it, that can be good or bad.

Dealing with long-term illness

Living with Anticipatory Grief while your loved one faces a long-term (chronic) sickness can be another big challenge because everybody's definition of long-term sickness is different. For some, it might be months while others live through this challenge for years. It might be nice to know the length of this season in advance, but even that knowledge would have its pros and cons.

An ex-Marine friend told me once that one of his sergeant's favorite exercises was to take the unit on a hike with no specified length. It was hard for the Marines to withstand the hike because it might be two miles or twenty. He said that not knowing was the point of the exercise. It created stronger Marines. Dealing with long-term sickness can feel like you're on a never-ending hike that you didn't sign up for.

Maintaining your relationship

You either pull closer to your loved one or drift farther apart. An unusual aspect of traumatic events like discovering that your loved one has a terminal illness is that relationships are hard to sustain at the same level. You either want to pull closer to the loved one or distance yourself from them, depending on your own personality. The goal is to maintain your relationship as closely as possible to the way it was before the diagnosis.

A couple of months after my business partner, Mark, shared with me that he had Stage 4 cancer, he told me something interesting. He shared that he had noticed that 95% of people either pulled away or almost smothered him with their concern. But the 5% who maintained the same level of their previous relationship were so rare that he loved them even more and eagerly looked forward to their visits and interactions. Strive for that 5% that brings you and your loved one even closer than ever before.

Making decisions

Use caution when making big decisions or life changes during Anticipatory Grief. Your atypical emotional state and mental fog can skew your judgment and cause you to make wrong decisions. If you think you need to make a major life change, ask one to three close friends for their input. When they give you their guidance, ask them why they believe the way they do. Their explanations could include things you had not considered and provide guidance that might make your decision clearer.

As Mark's health declined, it fell on me to make business decisions by myself including marketing, product creation, and special promotions. I had several product ideas I considered adding to the product line, but after pondering each idea, I decided to maintain the business and make changes a year or so down the road. Later I was glad I made that decision because the market changed, and if I had gone with my initial plans, I would have endangered the business's future success.

Being respectful

Ask before you do things, even if you're willing to do them. The goal is to be respectful. If you are spending extended periods of time with your loved one, you will probably be together at a mealtime, whether you're at their home or in the hospital. You could be called on to prepare a meal or snack for them. Your loved one might have special dietary requirements or restrictions, and if so, they will probably tell you what they need. So, what do you do about your own needs? You need to eat as well. When you find yourself in this position, be courteous to your loved one and ask them what they would like you to do. "Would you prefer I sit with you while you eat, eat with you, or eat in another room?"

While visiting Mark at home during his prolonged illness, a good friend and I brought ingredients to make a meal while we were there. When the meal was ready, we both ate in the kitchen, leaving Mark to watch TV in the living room. But Mark's feelings were hurt because he did not get to see the chicken enchiladas that we were eating. Even though he had a feeding tube, he still wanted to see what we were eating. I won't repeat that mistake.

Handling emotions

You just want it to be all over, whatever the outcome is. There is no shame in wanting the situation to be over. You might even find yourself praying that your loved one will "go home to heaven" sooner to alleviate their suffering. Then you might feel guilty for even having those thoughts. Your feelings are perfectly normal. God understands your pain and suffering just as He understands your loved one's pain and suffering.

It is typically more appropriate to pray for healing, comfort, and peace for your loved one. However, it's crucial to remember that God's ultimate plan and purpose may not always align with your desires or expectations. You must trust in His sovereignty and acknowledge that He knows what is best for each person, including when it is time for them to enter eternity. You can fervently pray for their physical and spiritual well-being, seeking God's will in their life. You can also pray for God's presence to be felt, for faith to be strengthened, and for them to experience peace and comfort throughout their journey.

Sharing your thoughts and feelings

If there's something you would like to say and you know that in the future you will wish you had said it, say it now. When you think about a loved one and the inevitability of having a finite amount of time with them, please consider sharing things that you have neglected or avoided saying. These can include "I love you," "Please forgive me," "You have made a difference in my life," "Thank you," "What I love most about you is …," "I forgive you," and "I will never forget you." You might also include your favorite memories with them and especially funny remembrances.

Why not plan a time when you know you will be together for a while and bring a list of everything you want to say? You will be glad later that you did. After getting permission, you might also want to record the exchange with your phone or tablet so you can listen to it later. Having their voice can be comforting later. Just ensure that you are ready to hear it later before you listen.

Laughing

Allow yourself to laugh. I realize it might sound irreverent or out-of-place, but laughing can help clear your mind, especially if you're in a particularly dark place at the moment. Keep a running list of things that make you laugh: memories, scenes in movies, quotes from a book, or maybe even an embarrassing moment. If you can't think of something to make yourself laugh, refer to your list. If you don't feel comfortable laughing in the presence of your loved one, wait until you have stepped away. Or if they like to laugh, why not work together to make a laughing list that you can pull from occasionally to create new experiences together?

In conclusion, there is no right or wrong way to deal with Anticipatory Grief. Don't berate yourself or feel guilty if you do something that you consider wrong. You and your loved one are experiencing so many emotions that your lives are anything but normal. So, give yourself grace, accept that there is no "perfect" way to go through Anticipatory Grief, and just be there for your loved one. Maya Angelou said, "At the end of the day people won't remember what you said or did, they will remember how you made them feel." Be the one who makes your loved one feel loved, respected, honored, and remembered.

My Prayer for You

Dear Heavenly Father,

I humbly come before You today, bringing the weight of my sorrow and pain as I seek Your divine comfort and strength for my dear friend coping with Anticipatory Grief. I acknowledge the immense struggle and anguish that comes with knowing that the loss of a loved one is imminent. I ask that You grant Your presence and solace to my precious friend who is walking this challenging path.

Lord, in this time of anticipating loss, I pray for Your loving arms to surround and uplift my friend. You see the deep ache in their heart, and You understand the heaviness of their emotions. I ask for Your divine grace to bring comfort and healing to their wounded soul.

Father, I pray for the gift of peace amidst the storm of emotions. In moments of fear, sadness, anger, and confusion, I ask for Your gentle touch to soothe their troubled hearts. May they find solace in knowing that You are the God of all comfort and that You are near to the brokenhearted.

Lord Jesus, You, too, experienced anguish as You faced the anticipation of the cross. You understand the depths of sorrow and grief. I ask that You walk alongside my friend who is grieving, offering them Your empathy and understanding. May Your presence be a guiding light, leading them through the darkness of their pain and into the hope of a new dawn.

Holy Spirit, I invite You to pour out Your peace that surpasses all understanding upon my friend who is grieving. Bring them moments of respite and clarity where they can experience Your loving embrace amidst their sorrow. Grant them the courage to openly express their emotions and the strength to rely on Your unfailing love.

Lord, I pray for a supportive community to surround my dear friend with compassion and understanding. May friends, family, and caregivers offer a safe space for them to share their burdens, providing comfort and companionship during this difficult journey. Grant them the wisdom to offer words of comfort and acts of love that truly lift the spirits of those grieving.

Lastly, dear Father, I pray for hope to be rekindled in the heart of my friend coping with Anticipatory Grief. Help them to cling to the promises found in Your Word, knowing that You bring healing and restoration, even during sorrow. May they find strength and peace in Your everlasting love.

I lift this prayer in the powerful name of Jesus, the one who understands our deepest pain and offers us eternal comfort, Amen.

19 The Unofficial Rules of Anticipatory Grief | 173

Support from The Word

"Man does not see what the Lord sees, for man sees what is visible, but the Lord sees the heart." 1 Samuel 16:7

For it was You who created my inward parts. You knit me together in my mother's womb. I will praise You because I have been remarkably and wonderfully made. Your works are wonderful, and I know this very well. Psalm 139:13-15

"As the Father has loved Me, I have also loved you. Remain in My love." John 15:9

Therefore, if anyone is in Christ, he is a new creation; old things have passed away, and look, new things have come. 2 Corinthians 5:17

I am sure of this, that He who started a good work in you will carry it on to completion until the day of Christ Jesus. Philippians 1:6

20
SELF-CARE

Self-care is an important part of our lives whether we realize it or not. When experiencing undue stress or anxiety, such as during Anticipatory Grief, it can be hard to focus on caring for ourselves while our brain is trying to handle physical, emotional, and mental challenges. But it is important to remember that self-care is not blatant indulgence like binge-watching an entire season of our favorite TV show, going on weekly shopping sprees, or living on comfort food. It is taking care of ourselves during this stressful time. It means we become our very own caregiver.

One common misconception regarding self-care is the idea that focusing on your needs is taking focus away from your loved one. You might feel guilty for taking time to prioritize your well-being, fearing it could be seen as selfish or neglectful. But that is simply not true.

By neglecting self-care, you put yourself at risk of becoming physically and emotionally depleted, which can lead to the above-mentioned physical, emotional, and mental challenges. Self-care is not indulgence, but rather an act of self-preservation that enables you to sustain your energy, focus, and attitude.

To overcome misconceptions surrounding self-care, you should remind yourself that prioritizing your well-being enables you to feel stronger and better emotionally, maintain clarity of mind, and interact successfully with others. When you are well-rested, emotionally balanced, and physically healthy, you are better equipped to face each day positively.

By understanding the significance of self-care, you can commit to nurturing yourself. Recognizing that taking care of yourself is not selfish but rather an act of love and responsibility, you can embark on a journey of self-care that benefits both you and your loved one.

Identifying your personal needs and boundaries

To effectively practice self-care, it's important for you to first identify your needs, interests, and personal goals. This involves taking the time to reflect on what brings you joy, what helps you relax, and what activities you find fulfilling. By understanding your own needs, you can better prioritize your self-care practices.

Physical self-care is an important aspect of overall well-being. You should prioritize maintaining a healthy lifestyle encompassing regular exercise, adequate sleep, and proper nutrition. Engaging in exercise not only improves physical health but also releases endorphins that can boost mood and reduce stress. Even short bursts of physical activity, such as taking a walk around the block, can be beneficial. You can also explore exercise options that can be done at home, such as using online workout videos or exercise equipment.

Anticipatory grief can be emotionally and mentally demanding, making it essential for you to prioritize your emotional and mental well-being. You should recognize and manage stress, anxiety, and depression by seeking support when needed. This can be done by confiding in a trusted family member or close friend, joining a support group, or seeking therapy or counseling services. Venting frustrations and concerns can help alleviate emotional burdens and provide a fresh perspective.

Practicing mindfulness and relaxation techniques can also be beneficial in reducing stress and promoting emotional well-being. You can dedicate a few minutes each day to engage in activities, such as deep breathing, prayer, or journaling. If time is limited, you could create a gratitude list and add one or two things each day that you are thankful for. These practices can help you focus on the present moment and alleviate overwhelming feelings.

Time management is crucial for you to create space for self-care. You can start by organizing and prioritizing tasks, breaking them down into smaller, manageable steps. Creating a daily or weekly schedule can help you allocate specific time slots for self-care activities and ensure you are not neglected. It's important for you to remember that taking care of yourself is just as important as taking care of your loved one.

In addition to organizing tasks, you can also implement time-saving tips to free up more time for self-care. This can include delegating tasks to other family members and using technology and automation tools to streamline processes. By effectively managing your time, you can create a balance between your responsibilities and your self-care needs.

The Anticipatory Grief tunnel can be a challenging time, which is why it's crucial for you to seek social support and build a network of people who can provide encouragement, understanding, and assistance. Having a support system in place can help you navigate the ups and downs of Anticipatory Grief and prevent feelings of isolation.

One of the benefits of seeking social support is having someone to share your experiences and emotions with. Talking to others who are going through or have gone through Anticipatory Grief can provide a sense of validation and understanding. You can share your joys, frustrations, and challenges with your support system, which can offer reassurance and empathy.

Making your self-care list

Pick at least one activity from each of the following life areas:

Physical Get plenty of sleep, eat nutritious meals, hydrate, exercise as time allows

Emotional Talk to a friend or family member, participate in a support group, vent frustrations

Mental Practice mindfulness, journaling, relaxation techniques, deep breathing

Spiritual Pray, read Scripture, attend Sunday School and church

Activities Sing, draw, color, soak in the tub, light a scented candle, play a phone game (app)

This list is only a starting point. You will no doubt have other ways to practice self-care. Make a master list of all these activities and incorporate them into your daily routine. If you find yourself overwhelmed or unsure of how to feel better, it could be that you are neglecting self-care. If this happens, refer to your list and add self-care back into your routine. Your body, mind, emotions, and spiritual well-being will thank you.

Just for caregivers

The remainder of this chapter is specifically written for caregivers. If you are a caregiver, I want you to know that I love and appreciate you. Caregiving can be a thankless job, and it can deprive you of the detachment needed to face the future. The suggestions I've included in this section are borne from witnessing caregivers' struggles. Please don't gloss over this section thinking that "you've got this." Although you may be strong, your responsibilities are many, and their impact extends into the future when *now* becomes a memory. Create good memories for yourself by being willing to take these suggestions to heart.

Caregiving is a loving, compassionate job that some step into, and some are pulled into. Wherever you find yourself on this scale, caregiving can exhaust you before you realize it. If you are caregiving for your loved one during Anticipatory Grief, your situation is a bit more challenging. It's important to recognize when you're feeling exhausted and as much as you are able, to prioritize your own well-being. It's important to emphasize again, especially for caregivers, that self-care is not selfish. It is a loving and essential responsibility that will make your job easier and help you remain loving while providing care.

Setting boundaries

Setting boundaries is crucial for ensuring that you have the necessary personal time and space to engage in self-care activities. Establishing clear boundaries with care recipients and other family members can help prevent burnout and feelings of being overwhelmed. You should communicate your needs and limits to others, and make sure to carve out specific periods of time dedicated to self-care.

The importance of self-care support systems

Caregiving can be a challenging and demanding role, which is why it's crucial for you to seek social support and build a network of people who can provide encouragement, understanding, and respite assistance. Having a support system in place can help you navigate the ups and downs of caregiving and prevent feelings of isolation and burnout.

Reaching out to family, friends, or support groups is a great way to build a support network. You can lean on your loved ones for emotional support, and friends and support groups can provide a sense of community and belonging. Online forums and social media groups dedicated to caregivers can also be valuable resources for connecting with others who are going through similar experiences. Online groups allow you to check in when you need encouragement and post when you need to vent. Even if you can't receive instant feedback, you can rest assured that the group members have been where you are and truly "get it." While receiving encouragement, you could hold the secret to a problem someone else in the group is battling.

Using professional resources

In addition to seeking support from friends, family, and online caregiver support groups, you should also explore the various professional resources available to you. These resources can provide guidance, education, and professional support to improve your caregiving experience.

      Healthcare professionals, such as doctors or nurses, can offer valuable insights and advice specific to your loved one's condition. They can provide information about managing symptoms, navigating medical appointments, and accessing appropriate resources. You shouldn't hesitate to reach out to healthcare professionals for assistance and guidance.

      Therapists or counselors can also be a valuable resource for you. These professionals can offer a safe and confidential space for you to express your feelings and emotions, and they can provide tools and strategies to cope with the challenges of caregiving. Therapy sessions can be an opportunity to develop healthy coping mechanisms and learn techniques to manage stress and burnout.

      Respite care services are another option for you to consider. Respite care provides temporary relief for you by offering trained professionals to step in and provide care for your loved one. This allows you to take some time for yourself, whether it's for self-care activities or simply to recharge. Exploring local respite care options and understanding how to access these services can greatly benefit you.

Dealing with guilt and emotional challenges

Guilt is a common feeling that can hinder you from prioritizing your own self-care. You often feel guilty for taking time away from your loved one or for focusing on your own needs.

However, it's important to recognize that self-care is not selfish but necessary for maintaining physical and mental well-being.

To overcome caregiver guilt, it can be helpful to reframe self-care as a way to better care for your loved one. Taking the time to recharge and address personal needs can actually improve the quality of care provided. You should remind yourself that you deserve and need self-care just as much as your loved one does.

It's also important for you to let go of perfectionism and self-imposed expectations. You often feel the need to do everything perfectly and meet unrealistic standards. By recognizing that it's okay to ask for help, delegate tasks, and prioritize your own well-being, you can alleviate some of the guilt and emotional challenges associated with caregiving.

Overcoming financial and time constraints

Financial and time constraints are common barriers that you face when trying to engage in self-care. Caregiving can be a full-time commitment, leaving little time for personal activities. However, there are options for you to overcome these constraints and find ways to practice self-care within your means.

You can explore cost-effective self-care options that fit your budget. This can include activities like taking a relaxing bath, reading a book from the library, or engaging in hobbies that don't require significant financial investment. You can also consider reaching out to local community centers or organizations that offer low-cost or free self-care programs.

Tailoring self-care activities to fit within a tight schedule is another effective approach. You can identify short periods of time throughout the day, such as during your loved one's nap or while waiting for appointments and use those moments for self-care. This can involve engaging in mindfulness exercises, listening to relaxing music, or practicing deep breathing exercises. Every little bit counts, and even small self-care practices can make a significant difference in overall well-being.

You should also consider seeking assistance from community resources or support services. Local caregiver support organizations may offer respite care programs or volunteers who can provide temporary relief to you. This can free up time for you to engage in self-care without worrying about your loved one's well-being.

It's important for you to remember that self-care is not a luxury but a necessity, and finding ways to practice self-care despite the challenges will ultimately benefit both you and your loved one. Remember the most important part of all: self-care is not selfish. It is necessary to emerge from the Anticipatory Grief tunnel as a healthy and whole person.

My Prayer for You

Dear Heavenly Father,

I come before You with a heavy heart, seeking Your comfort and guidance for my precious friend who is dealing with Anticipatory Grief. I lift to You my friend who is in need of self-care during this challenging time. I recognize that amidst the pain and turmoil, it is important for them to attend to their own emotional, physical, mental, and spiritual needs. Grant them the strength and wisdom to prioritize their well-being.

Loving God, I ask that You help them find moments of respite and rejuvenation even during their grief. Teach them to recognize when they need to take a step back and grant them the courage to do so without guilt. Remind them that self-care is not selfish but necessary for their own well-being.

Lord, grant them the ability to nourish their bodies with healthy food, exercise, and restful sleep. Provide them with perseverance to maintain healthy habits despite the emotional toll they face. Surround them with supportive individuals who can help, enabling them to take moments to care for themselves without feeling overwhelmed.

Father, I ask that You guard their heart and mind against the weight of Anticipatory Grief. Protect them from excessive worry, anxiety, and feelings of helplessness. Grant them moments of peace and stillness, allowing them to find peace in Your presence. Fill them with Your comforting and healing love, reminding them that they are not alone in their struggles.

Lord Jesus, You invite us to cast our burdens upon You, for Your yoke is easy and Your burden is light. Teach them to cast their anxieties, worries, and grief upon You, finding rest for their weary soul. Lead them to moments of quiet prayer and reflection, where they can find strength, hope, and renewed faith in Your promises.

Holy Spirit, remind them of the importance of seeking support from others. Guide them to connect with friends, support groups, or professionals who can provide a listening ear and guidance. Help them to express their emotions and experience the healing power of shared grief and understanding.

Father, I pray that You grant them moments of joy and respite amidst their grief. May they find solace in the beauty of nature, the laughter of loved ones, and the small blessings that surround them. Renew their spirit, infuse them with hope, and remind them of the preciousness of life.

I offer this prayer in the name of Jesus, my Comforter and Restorer, Amen.

Support from The Word

"Man does not see what the Lord sees, for man sees what is visible, but the Lord sees the heart." 1 Samuel 16:7

For it was You who created my inward parts. You knit me together in my mother's womb. I will praise You because I have been remarkably and wonderfully made. Your works are wonderful, and I know this very well. Psalm 139:13-14

"As the Father has loved Me, I have also loved you. Remain in My love." John 15:9

For you are His creation, created in Christ Jesus for good works, which God prepared ahead of time so that you should walk in them. Ephesians 2:10

I am sure of this, that He who started a good work in you will carry it on to completion until the day of Christ Jesus. Philippians 1:6

Part 5
Spiritual Challenges

Although anticipatory grief can shake
your spiritual foundations, and even lead you
to question your beliefs, in the end it can
strengthen your love for and understanding
of God's divine plan for your life.
— Cindi Dawson

hen I was in the fifth grade, something very scary happened to my family. My dad was working on our car and, needing a part, headed to the auto

parts store. It was such a quick errand that he didn't even let us know he was going. He planned to be back in less than 10 minutes, so he thought there was no need. When the phone rang with news that Daddy was being transported by ambulance to the hospital after a serious car accident, we were shocked. I remember one of us even went to the window to verify that he was not outside.

There's no other way to say it. The Anticipatory Grief tunnel is dark and scary. You didn't ask for it, you didn't expect it, and you don't want it, but it's there. You're going through it with no light. You just have to plod through it. And to make it even worse, you don't know how to respond or feel better. You're not sure if your feelings, thoughts, and physical sensations are brought on by the Anticipatory Grief or an equally serious problem.

That's how we felt when we received the news of Daddy's car accident. So, my mother, sisters, and I huddled in a circle and prayed for the doctors and Daddy's recovery. When Daddy passed the critical stage and we knew he was coming home from the hospital in a few days, my sisters and I decided to do something special for his homecoming. My dad came from a gifted, musical family. And my sisters and I had inherited the gift of music, playing instruments and singing together for a long time, but we wanted to surprise him with something above and beyond our previous musical experiences. So, we picked out two hymns in 3-part harmony and learned them especially for Daddy. We practiced a lot to ensure the harmony and blend were just right.

Working on these songs took the emphasis off ourselves and the sadness we were going through. It shifted our focus to something exciting. Even the words of the songs strengthened our faith that Daddy would get better. It gave us something to look forward to and that, in turn, encouraged us to practice harder. The Anticipatory Grief tunnel is very dark, and it can be hard to find something that will make you feel better, that encourages you to keep going. But if you look at what you have, whether tangible or intangible, you can find something that you can focus on.

The day finally came for Daddy to come home from the hospital, and we were both excited and scared. Once he was settled in his easy chair, we shared that we had a surprise for him. Then we sang Beneath the Cross of Jesus and The Solid Rock Medley. We hadn't been singing for very long when tears started rolling down his cheeks. While it was a bit challenging to sing while he was crying, we finished both songs and gently hugged him. We achieved our goal of surprising him. What a happy day! That day started a decades-long journey of singing trios and later quartets when my youngest sister was a bit older. While Daddy had a long road to recovery, we were glad we were able to contribute to a happy homecoming.

Although Daddy's wreck was a dark time, singing with my sisters brought something new and happy into our family's future. I'm so thankful that it did. While you are navigating the Anticipatory Grief tunnel, find a way that you can turn your dark journey into a joyous new part of your life. It will help you focus on something besides your current situation and provide hope for you to cope with your challenges while on the journey.

21
Anger at God

When you receive bad news, do you get mad? I can honestly say that sometimes I do and sometimes I don't. It depends on the news. When you first get the news about your loved one's situation, you might get mad. I got mad when I got the news about my mother's vascular dementia and again when I got the news about my business partner's cancer. I think I felt my views about justice, predictability, and fairness were challenged. The news in both circumstances made me feel unbalanced and vulnerable, so I took it out on an undefined vague person and got mad.

Looking at this explanation through spiritual eyes, it makes sense. Most people believe that God is all-knowing, all-powerful, and all-loving. And if you're a Christian, you hold fast to these beliefs. So, when God throws you a curve with devastating news, it's hard to rationalize this news with your image of God. You ask yourself lots of questions:

Why did God allow this to happen?
How could He do this?
Why didn't this happen to someone else?
Does He really love me?
Does He even care about me?
Why should I care about Him?
WHY DID YOU DO THIS TO ME?

Is it a sin to be angry at God?

No; expressing anger towards God is not a sin. However, it is important to be mindful of how you act on that anger as it can lead to problems. Self-control is a key aspect of spiritual maturity, as stated in Galatians 5:23, which is a part of the Fruit of the Spirit. For instance, Psalm 4:4 advises you to be angry but not to sin, suggesting that you should reflect on your feelings and find stillness within yourself.

A good example of someone who expressed anger towards God is Job. When he felt confused and angry, he sought an explanation from God. Job's outburst depicts a form of worship where you are honest about your emotions. God understood Job's feelings and addressed his outburst by redirecting his attention to His own goodness, rather than solely focusing on Job's personal pain.

These types of emotionally charged expressions to God are entirely appropriate, as demonstrated by people such as Jeremiah, King David, and even Jesus. Jeremiah expressed his emotions through an entire book in the Bible. King David wrote several Psalms where he cried out to God for protection and deliverance. Jesus, too, cried out to God while hanging on the cross, questioning why he was forsaken.

The key to understanding these orthodox emotions lies in the spiritual aspect Are you walking according to the Spirit's guidance? If so, you can be confident that your emotions align with God's emotions.

So, how can you get over your anger at God? How can you continue to trust Him? How can you regain your relationship with Him? To be honest, this can be a challenge, but it can be done.

If you're struggling with feelings of anger or frustration towards God, you're not alone. It's common for people to experience these emotions at some point in their lives, especially during challenging times like Anticipatory Grief. However, it's essential to address these feelings and find ways to regain a sense of peace.

Overcoming your anger

Here are some ways to navigate through your anger towards God and find solace in your relationship with Him.

Acknowledge your emotions. It's important to recognize and accept your feelings of anger towards God. Suppressing these emotions can worsen your mental and emotional well-being. Remember that God understands and can handle your emotions, so don't feel guilty for feeling angry.

Seek support. Finding someone to talk to can be tremendously helpful. Reach out to a trusted friend, family member, or spiritual leader who can provide guidance and a listening ear. They can offer valuable perspectives and comforting words, and help you process your anger in a healthy way.

Express yourself honestly to God. Don't be afraid to express your anger to God. Be honest with Him about your emotions, frustrations, and disappointments. Share your thoughts through prayers, writing in a journal, or any other creative outlet that allows you to convey your feelings. Remember, God is a loving and compassionate listener.

Think about your expectations. Take a moment to analyze your expectations of God. It's common for people to have certain visions of how God should intervene in their lives. However, these expectations can sometimes be unrealistic. Reflect on whether or not your anger stems from unmet expectations and try to develop a more realistic perspective of God's role in your life.

Look at the bigger picture. During times of anger, it can be challenging to see beyond your immediate circumstances. Take a step back and broaden your perspective. Consider the times when God has been present in your life, provided guidance, or offered blessings. Reflecting on these moments can help restore your faith and trust in God's plan.

Seek guidance from Scripture. Turn to Scriptures to find guidance and comfort. Reading stories of those who faced hardship and overcame their anger towards God can provide hope and inspiration. The Bible offers numerous examples of people struggling with anger but finding solace and a renewed relationship with God.

Practice self-care. Don't neglect your own well-being during this challenging time. Engage in activities that nurture your body, mind, and soul. This can include practicing self-compassion, enjoying hobbies you love, seeking professional counseling, or joining support groups where you can connect with others who have experienced similar emotions.

Feeling anger towards God is a common experience during times of hardship, but it doesn't have to consume you and move you away from His love. By acknowledging and expressing your emotions honestly, seeking support, and exploring alternative perspectives, you can find solace and forge a deeper connection with God. Remember, God is always ready to listen to you, understand you, and guide you towards healing and peace.

My Prayer for You

Loving and merciful Father,

I humbly come before You today, knowing that You are a God who understands my deepest emotions and struggles. I lift to You my precious friend who is coping with Anticipatory Grief, specifically wrestling with anger towards You. I acknowledge that anger towards You is a complex and raw emotion that arises from the depths of pain and loss. I ask for Your compassion, understanding, and healing touch upon their wounded heart.

Lord, I recognize that it can be challenging to comprehend the ways in which You work and the reasons behind grief. I bring before You my friend who is angry at You, questioning the circumstances that have caused them such immense pain and sorrow. Grant them the courage to express their anger honestly and to pour out their heart before You.

Father, I ask for Your divine presence to surround them, offering comfort and peace during their anger. Help them to find solace and understanding through their dialogue with You. Lord, You invite us to come to You with doubts and questions, so I ask that You meet them in their anger. Help them to wrestle with their emotions and lead them to a place of reconciliation and healing.

Lord Jesus, You, too, experienced the depths of anguish and anger as You cried out on the cross, "My God, my God, why have You forsaken me?" You understand the pain of feeling abandoned and betrayed by the Father. Be near to my friend who is angry at You, for You are the ultimate source of understanding and empathy.

Holy Spirit, I ask for Your comforting presence in their spiritual journey. Soften their hearts and open their eyes to Your love, even as they struggle to comprehend Your ways. Shine Your light upon their anger, bringing understanding and healing. Grant them the strength to surrender their anger to you, allowing the transformative power of Your love to bring them hope and peace.

Father, I pray for a revelation of Your divine purposes within their pain. Give them glimpses of Your goodness and faithfulness, even when they struggle to see it. Help them to trust in Your sovereignty, knowing that You are working all things for their ultimate good, even amidst their anger and confusion.

Lord, I acknowledge that anger towards You is not easy, and it may take time for healing and reconciliation to occur. I ask for Your patience and grace to sustain my dear friend in their journey towards spiritual renewal and a restored relationship with You.

I offer this prayer in the name of Jesus, my Savior and Redeemer, Amen.

Support from The Word

The LORD is the One who will go before you. He will be with you; He will not leave you or forsake you. Do not be afraid or discouraged. Deuteronomy 31:8

Haven't I commanded you, be strong and courageous? Do not be afraid or discouraged, for the LORD your God is with you wherever you go. Joshua 1:9

Refrain from anger and give up your rage; do not be agitated—it can only bring harm. For evildoers will be destroyed, but those who put their hope in the LORD will inherit the land. Psalm 37:8-9

Don't let your spirit rush to be angry, for anger abides in the heart of fools. Ecclesiastes 7:9

May mercy, peace, and love be multiplied to you. Jude 1:2

22
Feeling Abandoned by God

In moments of despair and adversity such as Anticipatory Grief, it's not uncommon for you to question God's presence in your life. You may wonder if you have been abandoned, left to face your struggles alone. However, it is crucial to recognize that the perception of being forsaken does not align with the truth of God's unwavering love and faithfulness.

In times of hardship, it is easy to become consumed by emotions and lose sight of God's bigger plan. Doubt and confusion can cloud your understanding, leading you to believe that God has turned His back on you. But the reality is far from that assumption. Scripture assures us that God is faithful, even in the darkest moments of your life.

When you go through trials, sufferings, or overwhelming challenges such as Anticipatory Grief, it's natural to question why a loving God would allow such experiences. In these moments, it can be easy to feel abandoned by God as you long for relief or answers during your pain.

We are finite beings trying to comprehend an infinite God. There are aspects of God's ways and plans that are beyond our comprehension. You see only a small piece of the puzzle while God sees the entire picture. His ways are higher than ours, and His plans are beyond your understanding. What may seem like abandonment to you could actually be God working behind the scenes, orchestrating events for your ultimate good.

Your expectations of how God should manifest His presence can also impact your perception of His nearness. You may have preconceived notions of what it means for God to be present, expecting miraculous signs or immediate relief from your suffering. However, God may be found in other places such as the comfort of a friend, the wisdom of a spiritual leader, or the peace that surpasses all understanding deep within your heart.

You may also have expectations of how God should fix this difficult situation. You may think He can heal your loved one and end their suffering immediately. And He could and might. But God's plan could be to heal your loved one by taking them home to be with Him. While that is hard for you to see now, ultimately it might be best for your loved one. It is hard to balance a limited human viewpoint with His infinite plan for you. And when your expectations don't match His plans, you feel abandoned.

God's love is not conditional, nor does it waver based on your circumstances. He is a compassionate Father who empathizes with your pain and suffering. The psalmist David experienced deep distress throughout his life, and yet, he ultimately found solace in God's love and faithfulness. In Psalm 22:1, David openly expressed his feelings of abandonment, crying out, "My God, my God, why have You forsaken me? Why are You so far from my deliverance and from my words of groaning?" Despite his cries, in Psalm 22:3, David recognized that God was still in control, stating, "But you are holy, enthroned on the praises of Israel."

Coping with the feeling of abandonment by God

So, how can you overcome this feeling of abandonment by God?

First, you need to realize that feeling abandoned by God while navigating the Anticipatory Grief tunnel is a common struggle that many Christians face. It's important to remember that our feelings are not always an accurate reflection of the truth. In times of stress and difficulty, it's crucial to cling to the unchanging truths of God's Word and rely on the promises He has given us.

Remember God's promises. Despite your circumstances, in Hebrews 13:5, the Bible assures you that God will never leave you nor forsake you. Even when you may feel abandoned, God is steadfastly present with you.

Seek God in prayer. Prayer is the means through which you can both speak to, and hear from, God. In times of distress, pour out your heart to Him, expressing your struggles, doubts, and fears. Trust that God is listening and that His peace will guard your heart and mind (Philippians 4:6-7).

Lean on His truth rather than allowing your emotions to dictate your understanding. You must remember that God's ways are higher than your own, and His timing is perfect. He may allow you to endure trials and tribulations to refine you, strengthen your faith, and ultimately draw you closer to Him.

Deepen your faith and trust in God. It's in these moments that you are reminded of your dependence on Him and that your strength comes from surrendering to His will. Instead of questioning God's nearness, seek Him even more fervently, knowing that He is using your circumstances to refine you and draw you into a closer relationship with Him.

Reflect on God's faithfulness. Remind yourself of the times when God has provided, protected, and answered your prayers in the past. Meditating on His faithfulness will anchor your soul in times of doubt and stress.

Surround yourself with fellow believers. Connect with your church community, seek support from trusted friends, and share your burdens with others who can offer encouragement and pray alongside you (Galatians 6:2).

Trust in God's greater plan. While it may be challenging to understand why God allows certain trials, trust that He has a better plan for your life. God uses difficult circumstances to shape and mold us into the image of Christ (Romans 8:28-29).

Embrace God's love and forgiveness. Despite your imperfections, God loves you unconditionally and is quick to forgive when you turn to Him. If you feel distant from God, confess your struggles, and ask for His forgiveness. Rest in His abundant grace (1 John 1:9).

Walk with Christ. While this doesn't exempt us from challenges in life, as we draw closer to Him through prayer, obedience, and a steadfast faith in His promises, we can experience His peace and guidance even during Anticipatory Grief.

Remember the ultimate act of love demonstrated by Christ on the cross in your moments of feeling abandoned. He willingly took on the weight of your sins, experiencing separation from God the Father for your sake. By embracing His sacrifice, you can be assured that you are never truly abandoned; rather, you are continually held in the embrace of God's immeasurable love.

My Prayer for You

Dear Heavenly Father,

In this moment of deep sorrow and Anticipatory Grief, I humbly come before Your throne of grace, knowing that You are the source of comfort, strength, and understanding. I lift to You my dear friend who is grieving in advance of a loss, acknowledging the turmoil they are experiencing, particularly in feeling abandoned by You.

Lord, my heart is heavy as I witness the pain and confusion that arises in times of grief. I ask for Your divine intervention, that You may grant them the spiritual solace and reassurance they seek. Help them to navigate through the emotions that oftentimes make Your presence feel distant or unreachable.

I acknowledge, O Lord, that Your Word assures us that You are a loving Heavenly Father who never leaves nor forsakes us, even in our darkest and most challenging moments. Yet, grief can cloud our understanding and blur the truth of Your unwavering companionship. Bring clarity and understanding to their heart, reminding them that no matter how they feel, You are always near.

Lord Jesus, as the resurrected Son of God, You intimately understand the depths of human pain and grief. You too experienced the feeling of abandonment on the cross when You cried out, "My God, My God, why have You forsaken me?"

(Matthew 27:46). You are not distant from their suffering, but rather compassionate and intimately present in their grief. May they find solace in knowing that You weep with them, that You understand their every sorrow.

Grant them, O Lord, a deepened faith in Your divine plan. Help them to trust in Your perfect wisdom, even when life's circumstances seem challenging and unfair. Remind them that in Isaiah 55:8-9, You tell us that Your ways are higher than our ways and Your thoughts higher than our thoughts. Guide them to surrender their feelings of abandonment into Your loving hands, knowing that You desire to bring about ultimate comfort and restoration.

Dear Heavenly Father, I ask that You pour out Your Holy Spirit upon them, comforting them through their sorrow and loneliness. Teach them to honestly pour out their doubts, fears, and questions before You, knowing that You are a God who listens and responds in love. May their prayers become a sanctuary where they find solace, where they experience Your healing presence whispering words of love and promise.

Lord, please surround them with a supportive Christian community. May their brothers and sisters in Christ offer open arms, tender hearts, and comforting ears, allowing them to feel the tangible love and care You provide through fellowship. Guide them to find strength and encouragement through the support of others who share their faith journey.

Father, remind them of Your unfailing forgiveness and incredible love. Help them to release any guilt they may carry and to receive Your forgiveness when they seek it. Let them know that Your sacrificial love on the cross covers every sin and failure, bridging the gap between their human frailty and Your perfect holiness. Assure them that they are forever embraced in Your forgiveness and grace.

Finally, Lord, as they walk this path of Anticipatory Grief, grant them a renewed understanding of Your unchanging, all-encompassing love. Shower them with the assurance that You provide for their every need, whether physical, emotional, mental, or spiritual. May they find solace in knowing that Your love is unconditional and that You will never abandon them.

I ask all these things in the name of Jesus, my Savior and Redeemer, Amen.

Support from The Word

May the LORD your God be with you as He was with your ancestors. May He not abandon you or leave us. 1 Kings 8:57

Now, Lord, what do I wait for? My hope is in You. Psalm 39:7

Because he is lovingly devoted to Me, I will deliver him; I will protect him because he knows My name. When he calls out to Me, I will answer him; I will be with him in trouble. I will rescue him and give him honor. I will satisfy him with a long life and show him My salvation. Psalm 91:14-16

Finally, brothers, rejoice. Become mature, be encouraged, be of the same mind, be at peace, and the God of love and peace will be with you. 2 Corinthians 13:11

I want their hearts to be encouraged and joined together in love, so that they may have all the riches of assured understanding and have the knowledge of God's mystery—Christ. Colossians 2:2

23
QUESTIONING GOD'S PLAN

Asking "Why?" is a typical response when experiencing Anticipatory Grief. "You might ask why this is happening, why it's happening now, why it's happening to your loved one, and why it's happening to you. Asking "Why?" is not new. People throughout history, including me, have asked why, but they didn't always receive an answer. I'm a "why" person. If I can understand why something is happening or why it is the way it is, I can cope with it and hopefully accept it. But if I can't find a clear explanation, I feel off balance and frustrated.

23 Questioning God's Plan

The story of Job is a well-known biblical narrative. It revolves around a man named Job who is described as righteous and blameless in the eyes of God. To read the entire story, go to the Old Testament and locate the book of Job. Job was an affluent and happy man, blessed with a large family, abundant wealth, and good health. One day, Satan challenged Job's faith, suggesting to God that Job was only loyal to God because of his privileged circumstances. Satan claimed that if Job were to suffer, he would turn away from God.

God allowed Satan to test Job's faith but did not allow Satan to kill Job. Tragedy struck Job's life as he lost his wealth, his children, and his health. Despite this immense suffering, Job remained steadfast in his faith, refusing to curse God or turn away from Him.

Job's friends came to offer him comfort and guidance, but they believed that his suffering was a result of his sins. They urged Job to repent and seek forgiveness. Job, however, maintained his innocence and questioned God's justice and his own predicament.

Throughout the story, Job engaged in a series of conversations with his friends, expressing his deep anguish and confusion. He longed for God to answer his questions and justify his suffering.

Eventually, God spoke directly to Job out of a whirlwind. God challenged Job's understanding of the world and reminded him of His sovereign power. Job realized his limited understanding and repented of his questioning. He humbly acknowledged God's wisdom and authority.

In the end, God restored Job's fortune, blessing him with even greater prosperity than before. Job's faith was affirmed, and he learned that suffering and hardship may not always be comprehensible to human understanding.

Just like Job, you are enduring multiple challenges as you navigate the Anticipatory Grief tunnel. And just like Job, you, too, are asking God questions about why you are going through this and why He doesn't make it all right again. You might feel that your prayers are not being heard or answered or that your situation is unjust, especially if you believe in a fair and just God. You might feel helpless, lose your sense of purpose, and even question your own faith. You probably feel like your dreams are gone and your relationship with God is on shaky ground.

But God never promised us that our life would be free of problems. He promised us that He loves us, that He has prepared a place for us if we believe in Him, and that we will have eternity with Him and with all those, including our loved ones, who also believe in His gift of eternal life. Even when we can't reconcile our current experiences with what God plans for us and our loved ones, we can rest assured that He is working things out according to His good and perfect will.

How to trust God's plan

Even if God doesn't choose to heal your loved one and restore your future to what you thought it would be, you can still learn to trust God through your current situation. Here are a few suggestions to help you accept God's plan while going through Anticipatory Grief.

Surrender to God. Remember that surrendering to God's plan does not mean dismissing your pain or suppressing your emotions. Instead, it means acknowledging that God is in control and trusting Him even in the midst of your grief. Surrender your worries, fears, and pain to Him, allowing Him to carry your burdens. If this seems overwhelming, keep a prayer journal of your doubts and fears. Then when each prayer is answered, make a note of the date and how it changed your feelings and relationship with God.

Seek His guidance in prayer. Prayer is a vital aspect of our relationship with God. Share your innermost thoughts, pain, and questions with Him. Ask for His peace to fill your heart and for wisdom to understand His plan. Remember, prayer is not just about speaking to God, but also about listening to His voice in stillness. After you have voiced your concerns, sit still, and listen for His guidance in dealing with your emotional challenges.

Seek comfort in His Word. Turn to the Bible for solace and guidance. The Psalms in particular offer profound insights into expressing grief and anguish and finding solace in God's presence. Meditate on verses that bring you comfort and remind you of God's faithfulness throughout history. Add verses to your prayer journal that have particular meaning and offer encouragement for you. You could also make a poster of the one that means the most and hang it where you can see it every day.

Seek support from your Christian community. Surround yourself with fellow believers who can provide spiritual encouragement and support during this difficult time. Share your struggles and pray together, allowing each other to be vessels of God's comfort and strength. Look for a small group within your church who know and love you and ask them to support you in prayer. Exchange phone numbers so they can text you encouraging messages or Scriptures that they think would brighten your day.

Embrace the hope of resurrection. As followers of Jesus, our hope lies in His resurrection. Jesus conquered death, and through Him, we have the assurance of eternal life. While Anticipatory Grief is challenging, remember that death is not the end, and there is hope beyond this earthly life. It can be difficult to remember this, especially when you're facing something as overwhelming as Anticipatory Grief. But keeping this in mind should calm your fears and give you a new focus.

Engage in acts of service and gratitude. While going through Anticipatory Grief, try to find ways to serve others and express gratitude to God. Acts of service can shift our focus from our own pain to the needs of others, reminding us of the love and compassion God has for His creation. Your church or small group might maintain a prayer list for people who are sick, are caregivers, or are facing big decisions. Sending a physical note or card can uplift you as much as it can help them with their current challenges.

Seek professional help if needed. If your Anticipatory Grief becomes overwhelming and affects your daily functioning, don't hesitate to seek professional counseling from a Christian therapist or counselor. They can provide you with additional tools and support tailored to your specific needs. Some churches have counselors on staff; however, if yours doesn't, you can find a local Christian counselor or even an online counselor who would be glad to counsel you via online meetings.

Remember, every individual's Anticipatory Grief tunnel is unique, and there's no timetable for healing. Give yourself grace, allowing the process to unfold naturally while seeking God's comfort and guidance. May God grant you peace and strength as you walk through this challenging season of Anticipatory Grief.

My Prayer for You

Dear Heavenly Father,

    As I come before Your throne of grace, I lift up our precious friend who is facing the heavy burden of Anticipatory Grief. I acknowledge that in times like these, when our hearts are heavy and our minds filled with questions, it can be challenging to trust in Your perfect plan. Yet, You are our source of strength and comfort, and we lean on You for guidance and understanding.

    Lord, I ask that You grant my dear friend the peace that surpasses all understanding, filling their heart and mind. May Your presence, which brings comfort and solace, be felt by them in this time of uncertainty and sorrow. Help them to surrender their doubts and fears, knowing that You are working all things together for their ultimate good.

    In moments when my friend questions Your plan, I pray that You would gently remind them of Your sovereignty and wisdom. Help them to trust that Your ways are higher than ours and that You hold their loved one's life in Your loving hands. Strengthen their faith, Lord, and grant them the assurance that, even in the midst of this pain, You are present and working for their spiritual growth and transformation.

    Father, I also pray that You would surround my friend with a community of believers who can uplift and support them during this challenging journey. Grant them the understanding and empathy of friends who can share in their grief and provide comfort to their weary soul. Help them to lean on the body of Christ for encouragement, wisdom, and guidance as they navigate through this difficult time.

    Lord, I trust in Your promises, for Your Word says that You are close to the brokenhearted and that You are near to those who call upon Your name. May my friend be reminded of Your unfailing love and may it bring them peace in the midst of their questioning. Help them to seek solace and guidance through prayer, knowing that it is through this sacred conversation with You that they can find clarity and renewed strength.

Gracious Father, I entrust my friend into Your caring arms. Provide them with the necessary strength, wisdom, and hope to face each day. Grant them a steadfast faith that can withstand the doubts and questions that may arise. Help them to continually surrender their pain and concerns to You, trusting in Your perfect plan. May their relationship with You deepen in ways they never thought possible during this season of grief.

I pray all these things in the precious and powerful name of Jesus Christ, our Lord and Savior, Amen.

Support from The Word

For You are my hope, Lord GOD, my confidence from my youth. Psalm 71:5

May you be blessed by the Lord, the Maker of heaven and earth. Psalm 115:15

May the LORD, Maker of heaven and earth, bless you from Zion. Psalm 134:3

Fear not, for I am with you; be not dismayed, for I am your God; I will strengthen you, I will help you, I will uphold you with my righteous right hand. Isaiah 41:10

I—I am the One who comforts you. Isaiah 51:12

24
Inability to Trust God

Do you have trouble trusting people? Do you have trouble trusting God? What about trusting God through Anticipatory Grief? To be honest, I have trouble trusting people which carries over into my relationship with God. I can say I trust Him. I can pray that He will show me how to trust Him. I can sing songs about trusting Him. But when it comes right down to it, trusting God is one of my biggest challenges. This area is one that I have been working on for a long time.

I wonder why people like me have so much trouble trusting God when there are so many Scriptures that encourage us to trust, so many examples of people in the Bible who demonstrated their trust, and so many opportunities to prove our trust in Him every day. I want to trust God, whether in the Anticipatory Grief tunnel or not. So, I decided to break this challenge into smaller pieces.

Reasons why you might not trust God

I made a list of reasons why I (and others like me) might have trouble trusting God. I hope and pray these reasons will give you some direction if you are facing the same challenge. See if any of these reasons ring true to you.

You might be afraid of the unknown. Anticipatory Grief can often leave you feeling uncertain about what lies ahead. The impending loss of your loved one brings about numerous questions and worries. It is natural to be afraid of the unknown and feel overwhelmed by the uncertainty of the future. This fear can make it difficult to fully trust in God's plan and surrender control to Him. Recognize that God is not only aware of the future but is also present in it. Psalm 46:1 tells us that He is our ever-present help in times of trouble, and Deuteronomy 31:6 promises that He will never leave or forsake us. Spend time in prayer, seeking God's comfort and guidance, and find solace in knowing that He is with you every step of the way.

You might be questioning God's goodness. During Anticipatory Grief, it's not uncommon for you to question why God would allow such pain and suffering. You may struggle to understand how a loving and all-powerful God can allow these difficult circumstances. This doubt can erode your trust in His goodness and make it challenging to fully rely on Him. During bouts of Anticipatory Grief, turn to Scripture and remind yourself of God's character. Reflect on passages like Psalm 34:8, which assures us that the Lord is good, and James 1:17, which reminds us that every good and perfect gift comes from above. Seek to deepen your understanding of God's sovereignty and learn to trust that even in the most painful circumstances, His plan will prevail (Romans 8:28).

You might be feeling betrayed. Anticipatory Grief often involves witnessing a loved one suffer. This experience can evoke feelings of betrayal by God. During these moments of doubt and struggle, take solace in the knowledge that Jesus Himself experienced deep sorrow and anguish. He understands our pain and suffering intimately, as shown in the Garden of Gethsemane (Matthew 26:36-46). Remember that God's ways are not our ways, and His perspective is infinitely wider and more profound than ours (Isaiah 55:8-9). Trust that He is working in ways we may not perceive, and in due time, He will bring about His purposes for our lives and the lives of those we love.

You might be disappointed in seemingly unanswered prayers. As Christians, we are encouraged to bring our burdens, fears, and desires to God in prayer. However, when prayers appear unanswered or the situation worsens, it can be disheartening. This disappointment can lead to feelings of doubt and mistrust towards God. It's important to remember that God's response to our prayers is not always immediate or according to our exact desires. His timing may not align with ours (Isaiah 55:9). In times of Anticipatory Grief, prayer becomes a way for us to draw nearer to God, trust in His wisdom, and seek His comfort, rather than just a means to obtain a specific outcome. Take comfort in knowing that God listens to our prayers (1 Peter 3:12), and even in the moments when we don't understand His plan, He is working for our ultimate good.

You might have lost your hope and purpose. Anticipatory Grief can lead to a profound loss of hope and a sense of purpose. It becomes challenging to see how God's plan and purpose fit into the pain and suffering we are experiencing. During these times, it's crucial to renew your mind with God's truth. Seek out Scripture that speaks to His overarching plan for humanity and the promises He offers to His children. Meditate on passages such as Jeremiah 29:11, which assures us that God has plans to prosper and not to harm us, and Romans 8:18, which reminds us that the sufferings of this present time are not worth comparing with the glory that will be revealed in us. Allow these promises to infuse hope and purpose back into your life, knowing that God is working even through your pain. Embrace the opportunity to draw closer to Him and seek a more intimate relationship with Christ, finding comfort in knowing that His love, presence, and provisions are sufficient for every need.

Ways to Trust God

God wants to have a closer relationship with you, and deepening your trust in Him is a great place to start. Focus on the following areas of your Christian life to strengthen your relationship with, and deepen your trust in, God.

Lean on prayer. Prayer is not only a way to communicate with God, but it's also a means of finding peace and guidance. As you enter into prayer, pour out your heart to God, expressing your deepest concerns, fears, and emotions. Trust that God is attentive to your prayers and will respond according to His perfect will and timing. Be open to the leading of the Holy Spirit as you pray, seeking His comfort, peace, and wisdom.

Seek God's Word. The Bible is a powerful tool for finding comfort, guidance, and encouragement. Take time to immerse yourself in Scripture, particularly passages that speak to God's faithfulness, love, and provision. Psalm 23 reminds us of God's shepherding care, Isaiah 41:10 assures us of His presence and strength, and Matthew 11:28-30 invites us to find rest in Him. Meditate on these verses, allowing them to penetrate your heart and mind, reinforcing your trust in God's character and promises.

Surround yourself with a supportive Christian community. It's essential to lean on the support and encouragement of fellow believers during times of grief. Connect with your church community or others who share your faith. Share your experiences and emotions with trusted friends and family, allowing them to walk alongside you in this journey. Seek comfort from those who can provide practical help and uphold you in prayer.

Reflect on God's past faithfulness. Take time to reflect on moments in your life when God has shown His faithfulness. Recall instances where He answered prayers, provided strength in difficult times, or guided you through challenges. Reminding yourself of how God has been present and active in the past will cultivate a deeper trust in His ability to sustain and comfort you in the present.

Create a treasure chest. Journaling or creating a gratitude list can serve as tangible reminders of God's goodness and love. Create a trust treasure chest, using a 3x5" file box. Use 3x5" cards to create brief notes (one on each card) about times when God provided for your needs or guided you through rough waters. When you need to be reminded, open the treasure chest, and read through your cards.

Surrender to God's Sovereignty. Acknowledge and embrace the truth that God is in control, even amidst your grief and pain. Even if you like to be in control, like me, allow yourself to surrender to His sovereignty, trusting that He has a perfect plan and purpose for your life and the life of your loved one. While this may not answer all your questions or solve every issue, it can provide a sense of peace and assurance that God sees the bigger picture. Acknowledge that His ways are higher than ours (Isaiah 55:8-9) and that He is working all things together for the good of those who love Him (Romans 8:28).

My Prayer for You

Dear Heavenly Father,

I come before You today with a heavy heart, seeking Your comfort and guidance for my precious friend who is grappling with Anticipatory Grief. I acknowledge that You are the ultimate source of strength and peace, and I ask for Your divine intervention in their situation.

Father, I understand that trusting You can be difficult, especially in times of deep pain and loss. Help my dear friend to surrender their fears, doubts, and worries into Your loving hands. Fill their heart with the assurance that You are with them every step of the way, providing comfort, understanding, and guidance.

Lord, I ask that You remove any barriers that hinder their ability to wholeheartedly trust in Your perfect plan. Help them to see that You are the Author of their story, and though they may not understand the reasons behind their current circumstances, You are working all things together for their ultimate good.

Grant them the peace that surpasses all understanding, knowing that You are in control and that their loved one is also safely in Your loving arms. Remind them that their faith in You allows for the unshakable hope and assurance of eternal life with You and their loved ones in heaven.

Heavenly Father, I pray that You open their spiritual eyes to see Your unfailing love and faithfulness. Strengthen their faith and help them to lean on Your Word, understanding that the Bible is Your inerrant message to guide and comfort them in all aspects of life.

Lord, I know that grief is a journey filled with ups and downs. Walk alongside my dear friend, being their constant companion in their times of doubt, sorrow, and loneliness. Surround them with a community of believers who will support and encourage them in their spiritual journey.

In the midst of their pain, lead them to find solace and strength through prayer. Help them to pour out their heart to You, knowing that prayer is the language by which they communicate with You and hear Your voice. May they find comfort and peace in Your presence, experiencing the healing touch of the Holy Spirit in their lives.

Finally, Lord, I humbly ask that You transform my dear friend's heart, renewing their trust in You. Help them to surrender their fears, doubts, and insecurities to Your loving care. Grant them the wisdom to embrace Your promises, for You are a faithful God who loves and protects us at all times.

I pray all these things in the name of Your precious Son, Jesus Christ, who overcame death and offers us eternal life, Amen.

Support from the Word

Those who know Your name trust in You because You have not abandoned those who seek You, Lord. Psalm 9:10

But I have trusted in Your faithful love; my heart will rejoice in Your deliverance. Psalm 13:5

Do not fear, for I am with you; do not be afraid, for I am your God. I will strengthen you; I will help you; I will hold on to you with My righteous right hand. Isaiah 41:10

The person who trusts in the Lord, whose confidence indeed is the Lord, is blessed. He will be like a tree planted by water: it sends its roots out toward a stream, it doesn't fear when heat comes, and its foliage remains green. It will not worry in a year of drought or cease producing fruit. Jeremiah 17:7-8

The Lord is good, a stronghold in a day of distress; He cares for those who take refuge in Him. Nahum 1:7

25
SPIRITUAL NUMBNESS

Spiritual numbness is an odd experience, and if you've gone through it, you understand what I mean. This was what I experienced during my bouts with Anticipatory Grief. It was so new and different; it was almost like an out-of-body experience.

Let me explain first that when I'm not navigating the Anticipatory Grief tunnel, I read my Bible daily, pray many times a day, whether consciously or subconsciously, and have Christian songs or hymns going through my mind. I will even sing out loud if I'm doing something mindless like washing dishes or the laundry. I attend church twice a week, once on Sunday morning for Sunday School and worship service, and on Wednesday night for Bible study and choir.

What is spiritual numbness?

Spiritual numbness refers to a state in which you feel disconnected, apathetic, or indifferent towards your spiritual beliefs, practices, or experiences. It is a sense of spiritual emptiness, a lack of emotional or experiential connection to your faith in God. When you are spiritually numb, you may not feel the same level of passion, enthusiasm, or resonance with your religious beliefs or practices as you did before. It can manifest as a feeling of being disconnected from God, a loss of joy or fulfillment in spiritual activities, or a sense of spiritual dryness. Spiritual numbness can be distressing for you, especially if you value your faith and seek a meaningful relationship with God.

Why are you experiencing spiritual numbness?

Anticipatory Grief is a complex and deeply personal emotion that can affect you in different ways, regardless of your religious beliefs. Here are a few possible reasons why you may experience spiritual numbness while navigating the Anticipatory Grief tunnel:

You might be emotionally overwhelmed. Anticipatory Grief can be mentally and emotionally overwhelming, causing you to feel disconnected or numb in multiple aspects of your life, including your spirituality.

You might question your faith. Anticipatory Grief often prompts profound questions about the meaning of life, the existence of God, and the fairness of the world. You may find yourself grappling with doubts or struggling to reconcile your understanding of God with the pain and loss you are experiencing.

You might feel abandoned by God. In times of loss, you may feel a sense of abandonment or distance from God. This can lead to a feeling of spiritual numbness, as you struggle to find solace or connection in your faith.

You might feel a loss of purpose or hope. Anticipatory Grief can shake your sense of purpose or future, making it challenging to find meaning or hope in your spiritual beliefs. This can result in a temporary numbness as you navigate your emotions and search for a renewed sense of purpose.

You might suppress your emotions. Sometimes you may unknowingly suppress your emotions as a defense mechanism to protect yourself from overwhelming pain. This suppression may extend to your spiritual life, leading to a sense of spiritual numbness.

You might change your focus. When you are experiencing physical, mental, and emotional challenges, it might be too hard for you to include God in your thoughts and schedule. It may be all you can do to breathe. This can result in spiritual numbness as well.

My spiritual numbness experience

When I received the word about my mother's vascular dementia and again with my business partner Mark's cancer, I felt like a door had closed with a bang. The door was not only shut, but it was also slammed shut and locked. My thoughts of God were gone. The music disappeared. The urge to read the Bible, pray, and attend church was just not there. I'll be honest with you. It was scary and not scary at the same time.

It was scary because my brain knew I was walking a different path from any path I had ever walked before. It was dark around me and I couldn't find my way. I felt like I was in an old black and white episode of The Twilight Zone, In the Fun House, and I couldn't find my way out. My life was one-dimensional—standing completely still with nowhere to go.

At the same time, it wasn't scary. My brain knew that God was there. My brain also knew that if I asked Him, He would guide me through this challenging time. But my heart didn't know those things, and that's why I should have been more scared. My brain had the ability to talk to God, but my heart wasn't in it. I'll confess something else to you. I stayed in that place for over two years – one while coping with my mother's vascular dementia, and one while coping with Mark's cancer. But God waited for my heart to step out of the tunnel and into a colorful life again.

I didn't want to go to church, but I went anyway. It was so strange because I could hear the words spoken to me, the lesson taught in Sunday School, the words to the worship and praise songs, and the words in the sermon. But the message was not there. The understanding was not there. It was almost like hearing the teacher's voice in a Peanuts® cartoon. (You know what I mean.) And when I got back home from church, I asked myself why I had gone. Most of the time I couldn't even remember what was said or sung. But I kept going.

My emergence from the darkness didn't just happen overnight. It was like my youngest sister described about going through her teen years, "I'm beginning to see the light at the end of the tunnel." I found myself talking to God, not praying specifically, but just talking to Him. And that gave me a tiny bit of hope and guidance back to Him.

I continued talking to God. Then one morning while I was in the shower, I remember hearing the faint piano notes of "It Is Well With My Soul" in my head. If you're not familiar with this song, I urge you to look it up and listen to it. It was one of my mother's favorite hymns, and I still can't sing it today without tearing up as I think of her and her love for the Lord.

Here are the lyrics to the first verse and chorus of "It Is Well With My Soul" by Philip Paul Bliss, composer, and Horatio Spafford, lyricist, written in 1871:

> When peace, like a river, attendeth my way,
> When sorrows like sea billows roll;
> Whatever my lot, Thou hast taught me to say,
> "It is well, it is well with my soul."
>
> CHORUS
> It is well with my soul. It is well, it is well with my soul.

How can you overcome spiritual numbness?

It would be easy for someone who has not experienced Anticipatory Grief and spiritual numbness to say, "Go to church, pray, read the Bible, and you will be all better." But for me, at least, I couldn't even summon the strength to get dressed to go to church. So, I've included the following ideas that will hopefully strengthen you in this time. Take one tiny step at a time.

Seek support from your loved ones. Surround yourself with caring friends and family members who can provide comfort and understanding during this difficult time. If you don't feel like leaving the house, text, email, or call someone just to connect for a minute or two.

Express your emotions. Find healthy outlets like journaling, art, or music, or just talk to someone about your feelings and experiences.

Practice self-care. Take care of your physical, emotional, and mental well-being. Get enough rest, maintain a balanced diet, and prioritize activities that bring you joy and relaxation.

Engage in acts of kindness. Practice compassion and help others. Volunteering or supporting a cause can provide a sense of purpose and fulfillment.

Connect with nature. Spend time in nature taking walks or enjoying peaceful surroundings. Nature can provide solace and a sense of connection beyond religious practices. Don't forget that being outside can happen at night when the stars are out. If you live in a large city, try finding a quiet place away from the city lights to enjoy star gazing.

Try gentle physical activity. Engaging in activities such as yoga, tai chi, or light exercise can help reduce stress and improve overall well-being.

Listen to uplifting music or podcasts. Surround yourself with positive and inspirational content that resonates with your values and beliefs. Find some inspiring quotes online, print them out, and hang them where they can uplift your emotions.

During my deepest Anticipatory Grief, I decided to try the following idea. While this is listed last, this is the suggestion that helped me the most. Choose a piece of clothing—dress, jeans, top, shoes, whatever you enjoy and is comfy—and wear it on days when you want to be surrounded by God and His love, but you can't bring yourself to speak with Him about it. Just knowing that you are "wearing" God's love can give you support and comfort during this heavy, challenging time. This verse explains why this helped me. Isaiah 61:1-3 says, "The Spirit of the Lord God is on Me, because the Lord has anointed Me to bring good news to the poor. He has sent Me to heal the brokenhearted, … to comfort all who mourn, … to give them a crown of beauty instead of ashes, ... and splendid clothes instead of despair."

Recovering from spiritual numbness can be a slow journey, taking baby steps. While these suggestions are not specifically spiritual practices, hopefully they can inspire you to take one step at a time to alleviate your spiritual numbness. It is my hope and prayer that you will gradually find your way back to God and the comfort and fulfillment a relationship with Him brings.

My Prayer for You

Dear Heavenly Father,

I come before You in humility and reverence, seeking Your divine presence and comfort for my precious friend. In this season of Anticipatory Grief, I lift their heavy heart to You, speaking to You on their behalf, focusing on the spiritual numbness they are experiencing.

Lord, I recognize that during times of grief, it is common for the spirit to feel numb and detached, causing confusion and an inability to sense Your presence. I ask You, O God, to touch my friend's spirit with Your gentle hand, awakening them to Your unfailing love and eternal truths.

Father, Psalm 34:18 assures us that You are near to the brokenhearted and save those who are crushed in spirit. I ask You to draw near to my friend today, filling their spirit with a renewed sense of Your presence and purpose. Break through the numbness that hinders their ability to connect with You in prayer and worship.

Lord Jesus, as You walked this earth, You encountered moments of deep anguish and sorrow. In Matthew 26:39 while in the garden of Gethsemane, we read that You felt overwhelmed and pleaded with the Father to let the cup pass from You. You understand the struggle of a numb spirit and the questions it can bring. May my friend find solace in knowing that You, too, have experienced the depths of human emotion.

Holy Spirit, I invite Your divine touch upon their spirit. Breathe life into the areas of their heart that feel desolate and disconnected from You. Soften the numbness that clouds their perception and hinders their ability to experience Your presence. Awaken within them a spiritual sensitivity to Your still, small voice and the leading of Your guidance.

Lord, I pray that You surround them with a community of faith that can walk alongside them in this journey. May their brothers and sisters in Christ offer support, encouragement, and a safe space to share their struggles. Let them find comfort in knowing that they are not alone but have fellow believers who understand and can lend a listening ear.

Dear Heavenly Father, I ask for wisdom and discernment for me as I seek ways to help my friend overcome spiritual numbness in this season of Anticipatory Grief. Guide them to engage in spiritual disciplines such as prayer, studying Your Word, and worship, even when it feels difficult and unfamiliar. Grant them the strength to push through the numbness, knowing that You, O Lord, are faithfully present in every moment.

Restore to them a joy and passion for You that surpasses their current circumstances. May their spirit be ignited with a renewed zeal to seek after Your heart and draw near to You. Help them to remember that even in their spiritual numbness, You are with them, working behind the scenes to bring comfort, healing, and restoration.

Lord, I trust in Your unfailing love and mercy. I know that You are the master of turning mourning into dancing, and You hold the power to bring beauty from ashes. I entrust my friend to Your loving care, believing that You will lead them through this season of Anticipatory Grief and bring them to a place of spiritual renewal.

In the precious name of Jesus, who conquered both numbness and death, I pray, Amen.

Support from The Word

Yet I am always with You; You hold my right hand. 24 You guide me with Your counsel, and afterward You will take me up in glory. Psalm 73:23-24

The Lord is near to all who call on him, to all who call on him in truth. Psalm 145:18

Fear not, for I am with you; be not dismayed, for I am your God; I will strengthen you, I will help you, I will uphold you with my righteous right hand. Isaiah 41:10

When you pass through the waters, I will be with you; and through the rivers, they shall not overwhelm you; when you walk through fire you shall not be burned, and the flame shall not consume you. Isaiah 43:2

Jesus Christ is the same yesterday, today, and forever. Hebrews 13:8

Conclusion

As we conclude our journey through "Courage in the Shadows," I hope you have felt my presence right there beside you, loving and encouraging you while navigating the ups and downs of Anticipatory Grief together. Writing this book was not only cathartic for me but hopefully empowering for you, helping you understand the hard things – the emotional roller coasters, the mental challenges, the physical aches and pains, the relational heartbreaks, and the spiritual questions that come with knowing we're losing someone we love. But it's also been about finding strength and light in those darkest moments.

Anticipatory Grief is a balancing act. On one hand, you're trying to soak up every last moment with your loved one, making memories that you'll cherish forever. On the other, you're bracing yourself for the goodbye that you know is coming. It's hard ... really, really hard. I understand what you're going through. But remember, it's okay to feel all those messy emotions – sadness, anger, confusion. It's all part of this complicated process. But you do have hope.

You're not alone in this. God is always with you. He will never leave you or forget you. And you have friends, family, and people in similar situations who love you and understand your Anticipatory Grief challenges. Don't hesitate to lean on them or to join groups where you can talk openly about your feelings. Sharing your story with others and talking to God about your challenges can ease your stress.

Remember that it's okay to find moments of joy and laughter, even when you feel guilty for doing it. Laughing and enjoying life doesn't mean you're forgetting your loved one or the seriousness of the situation. It means you're living fully, making the most of the time you have, which is so important. These moments of enjoyment strengthen you to make it through the next challenge, no matter what it is.

If you are a Christian, keep that connection strong. Prayer, meditation, reading the Bible, or spending time with fellow Christians can bring a lot of peace and hope. Reaching out to God and others often brings comfort and a sense of not being alone in your struggles.

I've said it before, but it bears repeating. Every feeling you're experiencing during Anticipatory Grief is valid and normal. Anticipatory Grief looks different for everybody. It's a personal path that's okay to walk at your own pace.

Keep taking things day by day. Use the strategies in this book to help manage your feelings and find balance. Whether it's writing in a journal, talking things out with a friend, praying, or just taking some quiet time for yourself, continue doing what helps you feel centered and calm.

I'm very grateful you chose to read this book, and I hope it's been like having a friend alongside you. May you continue to find strength and comfort in the days ahead, and always remember, there's light even on the darkest days.

I couldn't end this book without one final word of encouragement for you.

My Prayer for You

Dear Heavenly Father,

I come before You today to lift up a dear friend who is walking through the shadows of Anticipatory Grief. In these moments of sorrow and uncertainty, I ask for Your comforting presence to envelop them. Lord, You are our refuge and strength, an ever-present help in trouble. I pray that You will hold my dear friend close to Your heart, where they can feel Your love and peace that surpasses all understanding.

Grant them the courage to face each day, knowing that You are with them every step of the way. Fill their heart with hope, not for the circumstances that they desire, but for the deep, abiding peace that comes from trusting in Your divine plan. Help them to remember the joyful memories, to cherish the love shared, and to find solace in the knowledge that Your love binds us together, in this life and beyond.

Provide them with a community of support, friends and family who will offer practical help and emotional strength. Give me the wisdom to know how to comfort them in a way that honors their feelings and their process.

Lord, in Your mercy, hear my prayer. Comfort my dearest friend as they navigate this difficult journey, and lead them into a renewed sense of Your purpose and Your unwavering love for them.

In Jesus' name, Amen.

Discovering Hope

Hopefully, the information and Scripture verses in this book have helped you. Before you leave, I would like to share one more gift with you—a gift that will keep on giving forever. That is the gift of eternal life. And accepting it is as easy as A-B-C.

A

A stands for Admit. Admit you are a sinner. Romans 3:23 says, "For all have sinned and fall short of the glory of God."

Although we would like to say we are perfect, the truth is that no one is perfect. We all make mistakes and we all sin. Sin separates you from God. And without God in your life, you will be separated from God forever.

B

B stands for Believe. Believe that Jesus Christ came to this earth to die in your place ... giving His life for you. John 3:16 says, "For God loved the world in this way: He gave His One and Only Son, so that everyone who believes in Him will not perish but have eternal life."

While it can be hard to admit that you are a sinner, here's some good news. Jesus came to this earth to help us. He willingly gave His life so that your sins can be forgiven and so you can spend eternity with Him in heaven. He loves you that much.

C

C stands for Confess. Let the world know about your belief in God and His power to save you from your sins. Romans 10:9-10 says, "If you confess with your mouth, 'Jesus is Lord,' and believe in your heart that God raised Him from the dead, you will be saved. One believes with the heart, resulting in righteousness, and one confesses with the mouth, resulting in salvation."

Here's the best news yet. To restore a personal relationship with God and spend forever with him, you need to confess your belief in God to God, to yourself, and to others.

To follow these steps, pray the following prayer aloud:

"Dear Heavenly Father, I confess that I'm a sinner and I ask for Your forgiveness. I believe You died for my sins on the cross and rose from the dead. I repent of my sins. I invite You to come into my heart and my life. I want to trust You and follow You as my Lord and Savior. In Jesus' name, Amen."

Now that you have made this decision and are looking forward to spending eternity with God in heaven, share your decision with your pastor or priest and friends. Find a group of like-minded Christians with whom you can worship, grow, and learn more about God.

May God bless you on your journey to know Him better.
Cindi Dawson

Scriptural References All In One Place

All scripture verses in this book are from the Holman Christian Standard Bible®, used by permission.

(Feeling) Abandoned by God (Spiritual Challenges)

May the LORD your God be with you as He was with your ancestors. May He not abandon you or leave us. 1 Kings 8:57

Now, Lord, what do I wait for? My hope is in You. Psalm 39:7

Because he is lovingly devoted to Me, I will deliver him; I will protect him because he knows My name. When he calls out to Me, I will answer him; I will be with him in trouble. I will rescue him and give him honor. I will satisfy him with a long life and show him My salvation. Psalm 91:14-16

Finally, brothers, rejoice. Become mature, be encouraged, be of the same mind, be at peace, and the God of love and peace will be with you. 2 Corinthians 13 :11

I want their hearts to be encouraged and joined together in love, so that they may have all the riches of assured understanding and have the knowledge of God's mystery—Christ. Colossians 2:2

Anger (Emotional Challenges)

The LORD is the One who will go before you. He will be with you; He will not leave you or forsake you. Do not be afraid or discouraged. Deuteronomy 31:8

Refrain from anger and give up your rage; do not be agitated—it can only bring harm. For evildoers will be destroyed, but those who put their hope in the LORD will inherit the land. Psalm 37:8-9

May the LORD, Maker of heaven and earth, bless you from Zion. Psalm 134:3

A fool gives full vent to his anger, but a wise man holds it in check. Proverbs 29:11

My dearly loved brothers, understand this: Everyone must be quick to hear, slow to speak, and slow to anger, for man's anger does not accomplish God's righteousness. James 1:19-20

Anger at God (Spiritual Challenges)

The LORD is the One who will go before you. He will be with you; He will not leave you or forsake you. Do not be afraid or discouraged. Deuteronomy 31:8

Haven't I commanded you: be strong and courageous? Do not be afraid or discouraged, for the LORD your God is with you wherever you go. Joshua 1:9

Refrain from anger and give up your rage; do not be agitated—it can only bring harm. For evildoers will be destroyed, but those who put their hope in the LORD will inherit the land. Psalm 37:8-9

Don't let your spirit rush to be angry, for anger abides in the heart of fools. Ecclesiastes 7:9

May mercy, peace, and love be multiplied to you. Jude 1:2

Anxiety and Worry (Emotional Challenges)

The Lord is a refuge for the oppressed, a refuge in times of trouble. Psalm 9:9

Anxiety in a man's heart weighs it down, but a good word cheers it up. Proverbs 12:25

"This is why I tell you: Don't worry about your life, what you will eat or what you will drink; or about your body, what you will wear. Isn't life more than food and the body more than clothing? Look at the birds of the sky. They don't sow or reap or gather into barns, yet your heavenly Father feeds them. Aren't you worth more than they? Can any of you add a single cubit to his height by worrying? And why do you worry about clothes? Learn how the wildflowers of the field grow; they don't labor or spin thread. Yet I tell you that not even Solomon in all his splendor was adorned like one of these! If that's how God clothes the grass of the field, which is here today and thrown into the furnace tomorrow, won't He do much more for you—you of little faith? So don't worry, saying, 'What will you eat?' or 'What will you drink?' or 'What will you wear?' For the idolaters eagerly seek all these things, and your heavenly Father knows that you need them. But seek first the kingdom of God and His righteousness, and all these things will be provided for you. Therefore, don't worry about tomorrow, because tomorrow will worry about itself. Each day has enough trouble of its own. Matthew 6:25-34

We know that all things work together for the good of those who love God: those who are called according to His purpose. Romans 8:28

Don't worry about anything, but in everything, through prayer and petition with thanksgiving, let your requests be made known to God. And the peace of God, which surpasses every thought, will guard your hearts and minds in Christ Jesus. Philippians 4:6-7

Brain Fog (Mental Challenges)

Then He replied, "My presence will go with you, and I will give you rest." Exodus 33:14

The LORD is the One who will go before you. He will be with you; He will not leave you or forsake you. Do not be afraid or discouraged." Deuteronomy 31:8

I will both lie down and sleep in peace, for You alone, Lord, make me live in safety. Psalm 4:8

May He send you help from the sanctuary and sustain you from Zion. May He remember all your offerings and accept your burnt offering. May He give you what your heart desires and fulfill your whole purpose. Let you shout for joy at your victory and lift the banner in the name of your God. May Yahweh fulfill all your requests. Psalm 20:2-5

Therefore, my heart was glad, and my tongue rejoiced. Moreover, my flesh will rest in hope, Acts 2:26

Decision-Making Fatigue (Mental Challenges)

I will instruct you and teach you in the way you should go; I will counsel you with my loving eye on you. Psalm 32:8

Commit to the LORD whatever you do, and He will establish your plans. Proverbs 16:3

Whether you turn to the right or to the left, your ears will hear a voice behind you, saying, "This is the way; walk in it." Isaiah 30:21

Do not conform to the pattern of this world but be transformed by the renewing of your mind. Then you will be able to test and approve what God's will is—his good, pleasing, and perfect will. Romans 12:2

If any of you lacks wisdom, you should ask God, who gives generously to all without finding fault, and it will be given to you. James 1:5

Familial Anticipatory Grief (Relational Challenges)

The LORD is a refuge for the oppressed, a refuge in times of trouble. Those who know Your name trust in You because You have not abandoned those who seek You, Yahweh. Psalm 9:9-10

The LORD is my rock, my fortress, and my deliverer, my God, my mountain where I seek refuge, my shield and the horn of my salvation, my stronghold. Psalm 18:2

The eyes of the LORD are on the righteous, and His ears are open to their cry for help. Psalm 34:15

I am afflicted and needy; the Lord thinks of me. You are my helper and my deliverer; my God, do not delay. Psalm 40:17

For I know the plans I have for you"—this is the Lord's declaration—"plans for your welfare, not for disaster, to give you a future and a hope. Jeremiah 29:11

Fatigue (Physical Challenges)

The Lord is my shepherd; there is nothing I lack. He lets me lie down in green pastures; He leads me beside quiet waters. Psalm 23:1-2

But as for me—poor and in pain— let Your salvation protect me, God. Psalm 69:29

You will keep the mind that is dependent on You in perfect peace, for it is trusting in You. Isaiah 26:3

For I satisfy the thirsty person and feed all those who are weak. Jeremiah 31:25

Come to Me, all of you who are weary and burdened, and I will give you rest. All of you, take up My yoke and learn from Me, because I am gentle and humble in heart, and you will find rest for yourselves. For My yoke is easy and My burden is light. Matthew 11:28-30

Fear (Emotional Challenges)

The LORD is the One who will go before you. He will be with you; He will not leave you or forsake you. Do not be afraid or discouraged." Deuteronomy 31:8

The LORD is my light and my salvation—whom should I fear? The LORD is the stronghold of my life—of whom should I be afraid? When evildoers came against me to devour my flesh, my foes and my enemies stumbled and fell. Though an army deploys against me, my heart is not afraid; though a war breaks out against me, still I am confident. Psalm 27:1-3

When I am afraid, I will trust in You. In God, whose word I praise, in God I trust; I will not fear. What can man do to me? Psalm 56:3-4

Indeed, the hairs of your head are all counted. Don't be afraid; you are worth more than many sparrows! Luke 12:7

Now you have this treasure in clay jars, so that this extraordinary power may be from God and not from us. you are pressured in every way but not crushed; you are perplexed but not in despair; you are persecuted but not abandoned; you are struck down but not destroyed. 2 Corinthians 4:7-9

How to Help Your Loved One (Relational Challenges)

But He said to me, "My grace is sufficient for you, for power is perfected in weakness." Therefore, I will most gladly boast all the more about my weaknesses, so that Christ's power may reside in me. So I take pleasure in weaknesses, insults, catastrophes, persecutions, and in pressures, because of Christ. For when I am weak, then I am strong. 2 Corinthians 12:9-10

Don't worry about anything, but in everything, through prayer and petition with thanksgiving, let your requests be made known to God. Philippians 4:6

Therefore, you may boldly say, The Lord is my helper; I will not be afraid. What can man do to me? Hebrews 13:6

Humble yourselves, therefore, under the mighty hand of God, so that He may exalt you at the proper time, casting all your care on Him, because He cares about you. 1 Peter 5:6-7

He will wipe away every tear from their eyes. Death will no longer exist; grief, crying, and pain will exist no longer, because the previous things have passed away. Revelation 21:4

Inability to Trust God (Spiritual Challenges)

Those who know Your name trust in You because You have not abandoned those who seek You, Lord. Psalm 9:10

But I have trusted in Your faithful love; my heart will rejoice in Your deliverance. Psalm 13:5

Do not fear, for I am with you; do not be afraid, for I am your God. I will strengthen you; I will help you; I will hold on to you with My righteous right hand. Isaiah 41:10

The person who trusts in the Lord, whose confidence indeed is the Lord, is blessed. He will be like a tree planted by water: it sends its roots out toward a stream, it doesn't fear when heat comes, and its foliage remains green. It will not worry in a year of drought or cease producing fruit. Jeremiah 17:7-8

The Lord is good, a stronghold in a day of distress; He cares for those who take refuge in Him. Nahum 1:7

Insomnia (Physical Challenges)

I lie down and sleep; I wake again because the Lord sustains me. Psalm 3:5

I will both lie down and sleep in peace, for You alone, Lord, make me live in safety. Psalm 4:8

You will keep the mind that is dependent on You in perfect peace, for it is trusting in You. Isaiah 26:3

Though the mountains move and the hills shake, My love will not be removed from you and My covenant of peace will not be shaken," says your compassionate Lord. Isaiah 54:10

Come to Me, all of you who are weary and burdened, and I will give you rest. Matthew 11:28

Lack of Motivation (Mental Challenges)

Commit your way to the LORD, trust in Him, and He will act. Psalm 37:5

Commit to the LORD whatever you do, and He will establish your plans. Proverbs 16:3

Let us not become weary in doing good, for at the proper time we will reap a harvest if we do not give up. Galatians 6:9

I can do all things through Christ who strengthens me. Philippians 4:13

Whatever you do, work at it with all your heart, as working for the Lord, not for human masters, since you know that you will receive an inheritance from the Lord as a reward. It is the Lord Christ you are serving. Colossians 3:23-24

Loneliness (Mental Challenges)

LORD, You have searched me and known me. You know when I sit down and when I stand up; You understand my thoughts from far away. You observe my travels and my rest; You are aware of all my ways. Before a word is on my tongue, You know all about it, LORD. You have encircled me; You have placed Your hand on me. Psalm 139:1-5

The LORD is near all who call out to Him, all who call out to Him with integrity. Psalm 145:18

A man with many friends may be harmed, but there is a friend who stays closer than a brother. Proverbs 18:24

What then are you to say about these things? If God is for us, who is against us? Romans 8:31

The Lord will rescue me from every evil work and will bring me safely into His heavenly kingdom. To Him be the glory forever and ever! Amen. 2 Timothy 4:18

Loss of Appetite (Physical Challenges)

Know that the LORD has set apart the faithful for Himself; the LORD will hear when I call to Him. Psalm 4:3

Listen to my words, Lord; consider my sighing. Pay attention to the sound of my cry, my King and my God, for I pray to You. At daybreak, Lord, You hear my voice; at daybreak I plead my case to You and watch expectantly. Psalm 5:1-3

Yet He Himself bore your sicknesses, and He carried your pains; but you in turn regarded Him stricken, struck down by God, and afflicted. But He was pierced because of your transgressions, crushed because of your iniquities; punishment for your peace was on Him, and you are healed by His wounds. Isaiah 53:4-5

But for you who fear My name, the sun of righteousness will rise with healing in its wings, and you will go out and playfully jump like calves from the stall. Malachi 4:2

Heal me, LORD, and I will be healed; save me, and I will be saved, for You are my praise. Matthew 9:35

Pain (Physical Challenges)

Be strong and courageous, all you who put your hope in the LORD. Psalm 31:24

For your hearts rejoice in Him because you trust in His holy name. May Your faithful love rest on us, Yahweh, for you put your hope in You. Psalm 33:21-22

I put my hope in You, Lord; You will answer, Lord my God. Psalm 38:15

For I know the plans I have for you"—this is the Lord's declaration—"plans for your welfare, not for disaster, to give you a future and a hope. Jeremiah 29:11

And not only that, but you also rejoice in your afflictions, because you know that affliction produces endurance, endurance produces proven character, and proven character produces hope. This hope will not disappoint us, because God's love has been poured out in your hearts through the Holy Spirit who was given to us. Romans 5:3-5

Problem Solving (Mental Challenges)

Cast your cares on the Lord and He will sustain you; He will never let the righteous be shaken. Psalm 55:22

Teach me Your way, Yahweh, and I will live by Your truth. Give me an undivided mind to fear Your name. Psalm 86:11

Come to me, all you who are weary and burdened, and I will give you rest. Take My yoke upon you and learn from me, for I am gentle and humble in heart, and you will find rest for your souls. For My yoke is easy and My burden is light. Matthew 11:28-30

My grace is sufficient for you, for My power is made perfect in weakness. Therefore, I will boast all the more gladly about my weaknesses, so that Christ's power may rest on me. 2 Corinthians 12:9

Do not be anxious about anything, but in every situation, by prayer and petition, with thanksgiving, present your requests to God. And the peace of God, which transcends all understanding, will guard your hearts and your minds in Christ Jesus. Philippians 4:6-7

Questioning God's Plan (Spiritual Challenges)

For You are my hope, Lord GOD, my confidence from my youth. Psalm 71:5

May you be blessed by the Lord, the Maker of heaven and earth. Psalm 115:15

May the LORD, Maker of heaven and earth, bless you from Zion. Psalm 134:3

Fear not, for I am with you; be not dismayed, for I am your God; I will strengthen you, I will help you, I will uphold you with my righteous right hand. Isaiah 41:10

I—I am the One who comforts you. Isaiah 51:12

Sadness (Emotional Challenges)

Even when I go through the darkest valley, I fear no danger, for You are with me; Your rod and Your staff—they comfort me. Psalm 23:4

Trust in the LORD with all your heart, and do not rely on your own understanding; think about Him in all your ways, and He will guide you on the right paths. Proverbs 3:5-6

Those who mourn are blessed, for they will be comforted. Matthew 5:4

For I consider that the sufferings of this present time are not worth comparing with the glory that is going to be revealed to us. Romans 8:18

Praise the God and Father of your Lord Jesus Christ, the Father of mercies and the God of all comfort. He comforts you in all your affliction, so that you may be able to comfort those who are in any kind of affliction, through the comfort you ourselves receive from God. 2 Corinthians 1:3-4

Self-Care (Relational Challenges)

"Man does not see what the Lord sees, for man sees what is visible, but the Lord sees the heart." 1 Samuel 16:7

For it was You who created my inward parts. You knit me together in my mother's womb. I will praise You because I have been remarkably and wonderfully made. Your works are wonderful, and I know this very well. Psalm 139:13-14

"As the Father has loved Me, I have also loved you. Remain in My love." John 15:9

For you are His creation, created in Christ Jesus for good works, which God prepared ahead of time so that you should walk in them. Ephesians 2:10

I am sure of this, that He who started a good work in you will carry it on to completion until the day of Christ Jesus. Philippians 1:6

Shock (Emotional Challenges)

But You, LORD, are a shield around me, my glory, and the One who lifts up my head. Psalm 3:3

He gives strength to the weary and strengthens the powerless. Youths may faint and grow weary, and young men stumble and fall, but those who trust in the LORD will renew their strength;

they will soar on wings like eagles; they will run and not grow weary; they will walk and not faint. Isaiah 40:29-31

Because of the LORD's faithful love you do not perish, for His mercies never end. They are new every morning; great is Your faithfulness! Lamentations 3:22-23

The LORD is good, a stronghold in a day of distress; He cares for those who take refuge in Him. Nahum 1:7

"Peace I leave with you. My peace I give to you. I do not give to you as the world gives. Your heart must not be troubled or fearful." John 14:27

Spiritual Numbness (Spiritual Challenges)

Yet I am always with You; You hold my right hand. 24 You guide me with Your counsel, and afterward You will take me up in glory. Psalm 73:23-24

The Lord is near to all who call on him, to all who call on him in truth. Psalm 145:18

Fear not, for I am with you; be not dismayed, for I am your God; I will strengthen you, I will help you, I will uphold you with my righteous right hand. Isaiah 41:10

When you pass through the waters, I will be with you; and through the rivers, they shall not overwhelm you; when you walk through fire you shall not be burned, and the flame shall not consume you. Isaiah 43:2

Jesus Christ is the same yesterday, today, and forever. Hebrews 13:8

The Unofficial Rules of Anticipatory Grief (Relational Challenges)

The LORD is a refuge for the oppressed, a refuge in times of trouble. Those who know Your name trust in You because You have not abandoned those who seek You, Yahweh. Psalm 9:9-10

The LORD is my rock, my fortress, and my deliverer, my God, my mountain where I seek refuge, my shield and the horn of my salvation, my stronghold. Psalm 18:2

The eyes of the LORD are on the righteous, and His ears are open to their cry for help. Psalm 34:15

I am afflicted and needy; the Lord thinks of me. You are my helper and my deliverer; my God, do not delay. Psalm 40:17

For I know the plans I have for you"—this is the Lord's declaration—"plans for your welfare, not for disaster, to give you a future and a hope. Jeremiah 29:11

Weakened Immune System (Physical Challenges)

Be gracious to me, Lord, for I am weak; heal me, Lord, for my bones are shaking; my whole being is shaken with terror. And You, Lord—how long? Turn, Lord! Rescue me; save me because of Your faithful love. Psalm 6:2-4

Turn to me and be gracious to me, for I am alone and afflicted. The distresses of my heart increase; bring me out of my sufferings. Consider my affliction and trouble, and take away all my sins. Psalm 25:16-18

Heal me, Lord, and I will be healed; save me, and I will be saved, for You are my praise. Jeremiah 17:14

Therefore, confess your sins to one another and pray for one another, so that you may be healed. The urgent request of a righteous person is very powerful in its effect. James 5:16

He will wipe away every tear from their eyes. Death will no longer exist; grief, crying, and pain will exist no longer, because the previous things have passed away. Revelation 21:4

What to Say (Relational Challenges)

The LORD is good, a stronghold in a day of distress; He cares for those who take refuge in Him. Nahum 1:7

"Your heart must not be troubled. Believe in God; believe also in Me. In My Father's house are many dwelling places; if not, I would have told you. I am going away to prepare a place for you. If I go away and prepare a place for you, I will come back and receive you to Myself, so that where I am you may be also. You know the way to where I am going." John 14:1-4

"Peace I leave with you. My peace I give to you. I do not give to you as the world gives. Your heart must not be troubled or fearful." John 14:27

Now may the God of hope fill you with all joy and peace as you believe in Him so that you may overflow with hope by the power of the Holy Spirit. Romans 15:13

Praise the God and Father of your Lord Jesus Christ, the Father of mercies and the God of all comfort. He comforts you in all your affliction, so that you may be able to comfort those who are in any kind of affliction, through the comfort you ourselves receive from God. For as the sufferings of Christ overflow to us, so through Christ your comfort also overflows. 2 Corinthians 1:3-5

Resources

Cancer

American Cancer Society
http://www.cancer.org
   The American Cancer Society is a nationwide, community-based voluntary health organization dedicated to eliminating cancer as a major health problem. They conduct groundbreaking research, provide information and support for those affected by cancer, offer prevention and early detection programs, and advocate for policies to reduce cancer risk and improve access to high-quality care.

National Cancer Institute (NCI)
http://www.cancer.gov

    The National Cancer Institute, part of the National Institutes of Health, is the U.S. federal government's principal agency for cancer research and training. They support and conduct research to prevent, diagnose, and treat cancer, while also providing comprehensive information on various types of cancer, clinical trials, and resources for patients and healthcare professionals.

Susan G. Komen for the Cure
http://www.komen.org

    Susan G. Komen for the Cure is one of the largest breast cancer organizations in the United States. They are focused on funding research, providing support for those affected by breast cancer, and advocating for improved access to breast health services. Komen also hosts numerous fundraising events and educates the public about breast cancer risks and prevention strategies.

Leukemia & Lymphoma Society (LLS)
http://www.lls.org

    The Leukemia & Lymphoma Society is the world's largest voluntary health organization specifically dedicated to funding research, support, and advocacy to find cures for blood cancers. LLS supports groundbreaking research, provides financial assistance to patients, offers educational resources, and advocates for policies that benefit patients and increase access to treatments.

St. Jude Children's Research Hospital
http://www.stjude.org

St. Jude Children's Research Hospital is a leading pediatric treatment and research facility dedicated to finding cures for childhood cancer and other life-threatening diseases. They provide care to children regardless of their ability to pay, conduct pioneering research, and share their discoveries with the global scientific community to advance the fight against childhood cancer.

Heart Disease

American Heart Association (AHA)
http://www.heart.org

The American Heart Association is the country's largest voluntary organization dedicated to preventing and treating heart disease and stroke. AHA funds cutting-edge research, provides guidelines for healthcare professionals, educates the public about heart health, offers support for patients and caregivers, and advocates for policies that promote cardiovascular health.

National Heart, Lung, and Blood Institute (NHLBI)
http://www.nhlbi.nih.gov

The National Heart, Lung, and Blood Institute is part of the National Institutes of Health and focuses on research, education, and prevention of heart, lung, and blood diseases. NHLBI coordinates and supports research studies and clinical trials, provides educational resources for patients and professionals, and promotes the development of evidence-based guidelines for heart disease prevention and management.

WomenHeart The National Coalition for Women with Heart Disease
http://www.womenheart.org

    WomenHeart is the only national organization solely dedicated to supporting women living with heart disease. They provide essential patient support, education, and advocacy to empower women to take control of their cardiovascular health. WomenHeart also trains women to become community educators and advocates in their respective regions.

Heart Failure Society of America (HFSA)
http://www.hfsa.org

    The Heart Failure Society of America is a professional organization focused on heart failure research, treatment, and education. HFSA aims to improve patient care and outcomes by promoting awareness of heart failure, supporting research efforts, providing education to healthcare professionals, and advocating for policy changes to advance heart failure care.

Mended Hearts
http://www.mendedhearts.org

    Mended Hearts is a national nonprofit organization offering support and hope to heart disease patients and their families. They provide peer-to-peer support programs, hospital visitation programs, educational resources, and opportunities for patients and caregivers to connect and share information and experiences related to heart disease.

Chronic Obstructive Pulmonary Disease (COPD)

American Lung Association
http://www.lung.org

The American Lung Association is a leading organization dedicated to improving lung health and preventing lung diseases, including chronic obstructive pulmonary disease (COPD). They provide education, support, and advocacy for individuals living with COPD, fund research, promote tobacco cessation programs, and work to improve air quality.

COPD Foundation
http://www.copdfoundation.org

The COPD Foundation is a nonprofit organization focused on improving the lives of individuals affected by COPD. They support research, provide educational resources, offer community-based programs, advocate for policies that enhance COPD care, and encourage individuals with COPD to be proactive in managing their condition.

National Heart, Lung, and Blood Institute (NHLBI)
http://www.nhlbi.nih.gov

The National Heart, Lung, and Blood Institute conducts and supports research related to heart, lung, and blood diseases, including COPD. They provide educational materials on COPD prevention and management, support clinical trials, fund research initiatives, and collaborate with other organizations to improve the understanding and treatment of COPD.

Alpha-1 Foundation
http://www.alpha1.org

The Alpha-1 Foundation is dedicated to improving the lives of individuals affected by Alpha-1 Antitrypsin Deficiency, a genetic disorder that can lead to COPD. They fund research, provide resources and support for patients, advocate for access to care, and work to increase awareness and early detection of Alpha-1- related COPD.

Amyotrophic Lateral Sclerosis (ALS)

The ALS Association
http://www.alsa.org

The ALS Association is the largest nonprofit organization dedicated to fighting amyotrophic lateral sclerosis (ALS). Their mission is to discover treatments and a cure for ALS, provide support and resources for individuals living with ALS and their families, raise awareness about the disease, and advocate for policies that improve the lives of those affected by ALS.

Muscular Dystrophy Association (MDA)
http://www.mda.org

The Muscular Dystrophy Association is an organization that focuses on not only muscular dystrophy but also other neuromuscular diseases, including ALS. MDA funds research initiatives, provides comprehensive healthcare services and support to individuals with ALS, and offers various programs to enhance their quality of life.

ALS Therapy Development Institute (ALS TDI)
http://www.als.net

The ALS Therapy Development Institute is a nonprofit biotech organization solely dedicated to the discovery and development of effective treatments for ALS. ALS TDI accelerates the drug development process through their precision medicine program, conducts research, and collaborates with academic institutions and the pharmaceutical industry to find a cure for ALS.

Les Turner ALS Foundation
http://www.lesturnerals.org
    The Les Turner ALS Foundation is a comprehensive resource for people living with ALS in the Chicagoland area. They offer support services, access to clinical trials, education, and specialized care coordination, while also funding research and raising awareness about ALS.

Project ALS
http://www.projectals.org
    Project ALS is a nonprofit research organization that funds innovative science, promotes collaboration among researchers, and advocates for increased ALS research funding. They focus on advancing promising therapies and finding effective treatments for ALS through pioneering projects and a network of leading scientists and clinicians.

Alzheimer's Disease

Alzheimer's Association
http://www.alz.org
    The Alzheimer's Association is the leading nonprofit organization dedicated to Alzheimer's disease and dementia. They provide support services, resources, and education for individuals living with Alzheimer's, their families, and caregivers. The association also funds research programs, advocates for policy changes, and promotes brain health awareness.

UsAgainstAlzheimer's
http://www.usagainstalzheimers.org

UsAgainstAlzheimer's is a national advocacy organization committed to stopping Alzheimer's disease. They focus on raising awareness, accelerating research efforts, and advocating for policy change to improve care, support, and access to treatment for those affected by Alzheimer's. The organization engages with policymakers, researchers, caregivers, and patients to drive progress in Alzheimer's research and care.

Alzheimer's Foundation of America (AFA)
http://www.alzfdn.org

The Alzheimer's Foundation of America is a nonprofit organization dedicated to providing support, resources, and services for individuals with Alzheimer's disease and their caregivers. AFA offers a helpline, educational materials, advocacy initiatives, and programs that focus on improving quality of life for those living with Alzheimer's.

BrightFocus Foundation
http://www.brightfocus.org/alzheimers

The BrightFocus Foundation funds research and support programs to fight diseases of the aging mind, including Alzheimer's disease. They provide grants for innovative Alzheimer's research, offer educational resources, and strive to raise awareness about Alzheimer's and related dementias to support prevention, treatment, and a cure.

Alzheimer's Drug Discovery Foundation (ADDF)
http://www.alzdiscovery.org

The Alzheimer's Drug Discovery Foundation is a nonprofit organization focused on accelerating the development of effective treatments for Alzheimer's disease. They provide funding, support, and resources for preclinical and early-stage clinical drug discovery research. ADDF plays a critical role in advancing potential treatments and therapies to ultimately slow or stop the progression of Alzheimer's disease.

Acknowledgements

Writing a book is an interesting experience. Even though the book you hold in your hand is a single entity, for everyone who worked to create the book, it has been a living process. And I would be remiss if I didn't thank everyone who had a hand in this book. It never ceases to amaze me just how much and how many are involved in writing and publishing a book.

So many people contributed to this process that I fear I will leave someone out if I mention everyone by name. So, to ensure that I say everything I want to say, I will thank people for the role they played in the book's creation, rather than name by name.

Acknowledgements

First, I would like to thank everyone whose loss brought me to the point of writing this book. My heart has broken so many times over the loss of those close to me that I reasoned that there were others who had endured this same experience. And that's how this book came to be. Family members, church members, and business associates brought meaningful and important parts to this book. While these experiences of anticipatory grief were not happy, they taught me valuable lessons that I will carry with me for the rest of my life. I love you all and miss those of you who have gone before me. It is my sincerest joy that I will see you all again.

To those who helped with the book's organization and those who allowed me to interview you, thank you for sitting for hours, listening to my questions and ponderings about everything from chapter divisions to spiritual dilemmas. And to my family for allowing me to use your stories to make the book three-dimensional. You all contributed to the final version of the book.

No book would be complete without beta readers, layout artists, cover designers, proofers, formatters, and last-minute error-catchers. Thank you for your part. And thank you to those who prayed with me through the book creation process, from its inception to its final publication.

This book has been a labor of love. It originally came to me in my sleep with a calling so strong that I couldn't get on with my life until I set aside time to make it a reality. I am not the same person I was when I started this book. This is the book I wanted and needed when I began my journey through the Anticipatory Grief tunnel. I'm glad I put everything else on hold and shared this book from my heart. I met so many of you along the way. Thank you for giving of your time and skills. I deeply appreciate each and every one of you.

For you, the reader, we haven't met in person yet, but I pray for you daily, understanding Anticipatory Grief but knowing that everyone's journey is unique. I pray that you will be supported and loved during your time in the tunnel. Thank you for taking time to read this book. I hope and pray that it has been and will continue to be a source of support and encouragement for you in the days ahead.

Before you go, I'd like to invite you to join me in the Anticipatory Grief Circle on Facebook. You can find it here: https://Facebook.com/groups/agcircle Because your free time and schedule can be unpredictable right now, participating in an online support group is probably the best way for you to give and receive support. Feel free to ask for and lend support, describing what helped you most and asking questions about what other people have discovered. This group is a safe place. Feel free to vent when you need to. I created this group just for you, and I look forward to meeting you there.

Endnotes

[1] Sheri Jacobson, "7 Warning Signs You Are Suffering from Emotional Shock," September 23, 2022, https://www.harleytherapy.co.uk/counselling/7-warning-signs-acute-stress-reaction-emotional-shock.htm

[2] Jennifer Berry, "Everything You Need to Know About Shock," November 11, 2019, https://www.medicalnewstoday.com/articles/326959#symptoms

³ Lawrence Robinson, Melinda Smith, and Jeanne Segal, "Emotional and Psychological Trauma," accessed September 1, 2023, https://www.helpguide.org/articles/ptsd-trauma/coping-with-emotional-and-psychological-trauma.htm

⁴ Sanjana Gupta, "Identifying and Coping With Emotional Shock," February 20, 2023, https://www.verywellmind.com/emotional-shock-definition-symptoms-causes-and-treatment 5214434# ~ text=Go%20somewhere%20where%20you%20feel,pets%20or%20familiar%2C%20comforting%20objects.

⁵ Leonard Holmes, "Sadness vs. Clinical Depression," May 22, 2023, https://www.verywellmind.com/sadness-is-not-depression-2330492

⁶ Madeline Miles, "It's OK to be Sad. Here is Why You Need Some Sadness and How to Use It," June 30, 2022, https://www.betterup.com/blog/purpose-of-sadness

⁷ Peggy Rios, "How to Cope with Sadness," February 26, 2021, https://www.wikihow.com/Cope-with-Sadness

⁸ Erica Cirino, "Why Am I So Angry," March 30, 2023, https://www.healthline.com/health/why-am-i-so-angry

⁹ "Anger," Mind, accessed September 1, 2023, https://www.mind.org.uk/information-support/types-of-mental-health-problems/anger/causes-of-anger/

[10] "Coping with Anger," SAMHSA, April 27, 2022, https://www.samhsa.gov/dtac/disaster-survivors/coping-anger-after-disaster# ~ text=Anger%20has%20many%20benefits%2C%20including,headaches%2C%20depression%2C%20and%20anxiety.

[11] "10 Healthy Ways to Release Rage," MHA, accessed September 1, 2023, https://mhanational.org/10-healthy-ways-release-rage

[12] "Worry," dictionary, accessed September 1, 2023, https://www.dictionary.com/browse/worry

[13] Henry Ford, "Worry and Anxiety: Do You Know the Difference," August 21, 2020, https://www.henryford.com/blog/2020/08/the-difference-between-worry-and-anxiety# ~ text=Worry%20is%20temporary.&text=Worry%20prods%20you%20to%20use,compromises%20your%20ability%20to%20function.

[14] Jamie Wiebe, "Am I Anxious? 6 Common Signs of Anxiety," last modified November 1, 2023, https://www.talkspace.com/mental-health/conditions/articles/am-i-anxious-common-signs-of-anxiety/

[15] Seth J. Gillihan, "5 Reasons We Worry, and 5 Ways to Worry Less," October 7, 2016, https://www.psychologytoday.com/us/blog/think-act-be/201610/5-reasons-we-worry-and-5-ways-worry-less

[16] Lisa Fritscher, "The Psychology of Fear," April 11, 2023, https://www.verywellmind.com/the-psychology-of-fear-2671696

[17] "Phobias," Mind, accessed September 1, 2023, https://www.mind.org.uk/information-support/types-of-mental-health-problems/phobias/symptoms-of-phobias/#~text=feeling%20unsteady%2C%20dizzy%2C%20lightheaded%20or,or%20tightness%20in%20the%20chest

[18] Louise Delagran, "Impact of Fear and Anxiety," accessed September 1, 2023, https://www.takingcharge.csh.umn.edu/impact-fear-and-anxiety#~text=Fear%20can%20interrupt%20processes%20in,intense%20emotions%20and%20impulsive%20reactions.

[19] "10 Ways to Fight Your Fears," NHS inform, January 4, 2023, https://www.nhsinform.scot/healthy-living/mental-wellbeing/fears-and-phobias/10-ways-to-fight-your-fears

[20] "Brain Fog," Dictionary, last modified November 2, 2023, https://www.merriam-webster.com/dictionary/brain%20fog

[21] Meghan Rabbitt, "Here's Why You're Dealing With Brain Fog and What You Can Do to Fight It," November 21, 2020, https://www.prevention.com/health/a34600381/what-is-brain-fog/?utm_source=google&utm_medium=cpc&utm_campaign=arb_ga_pre_md_dsa_prog_mix_us_20398549654&gclid=CjwKCAjwxOymBhAFEiwAnodBLM-7krk_EdJw-trCSapphevswldMXvDbbiDrlqLLc8tWpdd9Pznb_hoC8wgQAvD_BwE

[22] "Long-term effects of COVID-19," NHS inform, last modified February 9, 2023, https://www.nhsinform.scot/long-term-effects-of-covid-19-long-covid/signs-and-symptoms/long-covid-brain-fog

[23] Arricca Elin SanSone, "Your 5-Minute Read on Fighting Brain Fog," last modified March 16, 2023, https://www.healthline.com/health/your-5-minute-read-on-fighting-brain-fog#avoid-caffeine-and-alcohol

[24] Megan Marples, "Decision Fatigue Drains You of Your Energy to Make Thoughtful Choices. Here's How to Get it Back," last modified April 21, 2022, https://www.cnn.com/2022/04/21/health/decision-fatigue-solutions-wellness/index.html#~text=Whether%20you're%20making%20breakfast,Leicester%20in%20the%20United%20Kingdom

[25] "How Stress Impacts Decision Making," Walden University, accessed September 1, 2023, https://www.waldenu.edu/online-masters-programs/ms-in-clinical-mental-health-counseling/resource/how-stress-impacts-decision-making#~text=There%20is%20a%20decrease%20in,needs%20to%20make%20logical%20decisions.&text=When%20the%20brain%20is%20under,prove%20to%20be%20more%20difficult

[26] Elizabeth Yuko, "9 Signs You Have Decision Fatigue and Tips to Help Manage It," last modified March 29, 2023, https://www.realsimple.com/health/mind-mood/decision-fatigue

[27] Jon Johnson, "What is decision fatigue," July 7, 2020, https://www.medicalnewstoday.com/articles/decision-fatigue#how-to-combat-it

[28] Kaiser Permanente, "Feeling Stressed from Making Decisions? Here are 4 Tips for Dealing with Decision Fatigue," October 10, 2022, https://healthy.kaiserpermanente.org/hawaii/health-wellness/healtharticle.tips-for-dealing-with-decision-fatigue

[29] Elizabeth Yuko, "Signs You Have Decision Fatigue and Tips to Manage It," January 11, 2023, https://www.mindpath.com/resource/signs-you-have-decision-fatigue-and-tips-to-manage-it/

[30] Traci Pedersen, "What Does Grief Do to Your Brain," last modified May 6, 2022, https://psychcentral.com/lib/your-health-and-grief#how-grief-affects-the-brain

[31] Megan Devine, "Grief Impacts our Brains," accessed September 1, 2023, https://speakinggrief.org/get-better-at-grief/understanding-grief/cognitive-effects#~text=Cognitive%20effects%20of%20grief%20are,might%20be%20misplaced%20more%20often.

[32] Zawn Villines, "Disordered Executive Function: What to Know," last modified October 12, 2023, https://www.medicalnewstoday.com/articles/325402#symptoms

[33] Careers in Psychology, "Type of Therapy - Cognitive Behavioral Therapy," accessed September 1, 2023, https://careersinpsychology.org/cognitive-behavioral-therapy/#~text=The%20ultimate%20goal%20of%20CBT,own%20interpretations%20of%20the%20world.

[34] "The Difference between Laziness, Lack of Motivation and Depression," With Chelle
A Fashion & Lifestyle Blog, September 23, 2020, https://withchelle.com/blog/2020/9/21/the-difference-between-laziness-no-motivation-and-depression#~text=Lack%20of%20motivation%20is%20essentially,have%20some%20elements%20of%20depression

[35] Scott Jeffrey, "The 8 Voices of Laziness and How to Overcome Them," April 10, 2017, https://psychcentral.com/blog/the-8-voices-of-laziness-and-how-to-overcome-them

[36] "Feeling Depressed and Struggling with Motivation? Build Momentum," Society of Behavioral Medicine, accessed September 1, 2023, https://www.sbm.org/healthy-living/feeling-depressed-and-struggling-with-motivation-build-momentum?gad=1&gclid=CjwKCAjwloynBhBbEiwAGY25dGVEKLR_aUUJz3vhpyHvcICL3MuwWtQzto5SL6tpZV5pV4CN1CUseRoCf60QAvD_BwE

[37] "Facts and Statistics About Loneliness," The Campaign to End Loneliness, accessed September 1, 2023, https://www.campaigntoendloneliness.org/facts-and-statistics/

[38] Emily Deaton, "Signs of Loneliness What To Watch For (And When To Worry)," accessed September 1, 2023, https://www.rootsofloneliness.com/signs-of-loneliness?expand_article=1

[39] Claire Asher, "Why do Identical Twins Have Different Fingerprints," September 18, 2021, https://www.sciencefocus.com/the-human-body/why-do-identical-twins-have-different-fingerprints-2

[40] Danielle Pacheco, "Grief and Its Effect on Sleep," last modified June 10, 2022, https://www.sleepfoundation.org/mental-health/grief-and-sleep#~text=The%20loss%20of%20a%20loved,the%20quality%20of%20their%20sleep.

⁴¹ Danielle Pacheco, "Sleep Disorders," May 16, 2022, https://www.sleepfoundation.org/sleep-disorders#~text=The%20collective%20term%20sleep%20disorder%20refers%20to,be%20symptoms%20for%20underlying%20mental%20health%20issues.

⁴² Ashley Marcin, "What You Need to Know About Insomnia and Grief," July 6, 2022, https://www.healthline.com/health/grief-cant-sleep#insomnia

⁴³ Hope Gillette, "Grief and Loss of Appetite What Is the Link," September 19, 2022, https://psychcentral.com/health/grief-loss-of-appetite

⁴⁴ Kati Blake, "What Causes Loss of Appetite," February 15, 2023, https://www.healthline.com/health/appetitedecreased#~text=If%20your%20decreased%20appetite%20persists,longer%20than%20a%20few%20weeks.

⁴⁵ Joanna Foley, "7 Tips for Eating When You Have No Appetite - And Foods that Might Help," April 3, 2023, https://www.goodrx.com/well-being/diet-nutrition/what-to-eat-when-you-have-no-appetite

⁴⁶ Courtney Yost, "10 Comfort Foods that America Loves," September 04, 2022, https://www.therecipe.com/10-comfort-foods-america-loves/

47 "Stressful Vulnerability How Anxiety Can Weaken Our Immune System," Choice House, September 30, 2020, https://www.choicehousecolorado.com/stressful-vulnerability-how-anxiety-can-weaken-our-immune-system/# ~ text=When%20you%20experience%20extended%2C%20prolonged,your%20immune%20system%20over%20time

48 Nadia Hasan, "6 Signs You Have a Weakened Immune System," February 16, 2022, https://www.pennmedicine.org/updates/blogs/health-and-wellness/2020/march/weakened-immune-system

49 "Six Tips to Enhance Immunity," About CDC, accessed September 1, 2023, https://www.cdc.gov/nccdphp/dnpao/features/enhance-immunity/index.html# ~ text=Some%20additional%20ways%20you%20can,and%20avoiding%20excessive%20alcohol%20use

50 Nisha Kikunga, "The Physical Pain of Grief 4 Things You Can Do To Help," accessed September 1, 2023, https://www.vorihealth.com/article/the-physical-pain-of-grief-4-things-you-can-do-to-help# ~ text=When%20you%20grieve%2C%20your%20body,lasting%20from%20weeks%20to%20months

51 Stephanie Hairston, "How Grief Shows Up in Your Body," July 11, 2019, https://www.webmd.com/special-reports/grief-stages/20190711/how-grief-affects-your-body-and-mind# ~ text=Intense%20grief%20can%20alter%20the,and%20physical%20aspects%20of%20grief

⁵² Alexander M. Dydyk, "Chronic Pain," July 21, 2023, https://www.ncbi.nlm.nih.gov/books/NBK553030/#~text=Chronic%20pain%20leads%20to%20significantly,for%20suicide%20and%20suicidal%20ideation

⁵³ "How to Reduce Stress Related Pain and Muscle Tension," Tri Health, accessed September 1, 2023, https://www.trihealth.com/dailyhealthwire/living-well/health-tips/how-to-reduce-stress-related-pain-and-muscle-tension#~text=Stress%20can%20hurt.,the%20shoulders%2C%20neck%20and%20head

⁵⁴ "Physical Symptoms of Grief," Marie Curie, accessed September 1, 2023, https://www.mariecurie.org.uk/help/support/bereaved-family-friends/dealing-grief/physical-symptoms-grief#~text=Strong%20emotions%20along%20with%20all,rest%20when%20you%20are%20grieving

⁵⁵ "Grief Impacts our Brains," WPSU, accessed September 1, 2023, https://speakinggrief.org/get-better-at-grief/understanding-grief/cognitive-effects#~text=Cognitive%20effects%20of%20grief%20are,might%20be%20misplaced%20more%20often

⁵⁶ Eileen Bailey, "What Is Stress-Related Fatigue," August 8, 2018, https://www.healthcentral.com/article/stress-and-fatigue

[57] Empathy's Grief, "Dealing with Crisis Fatigue," accessed September 1, 2023, https://www.empathy.com/grief/dealing-with-crisis-fatigue

[58] "How to Overcome Grief's Health-Damaging Effects," Harvard Health Publishing, February 15, 2021, https://www.health.harvard.edu/mind-and-mood/how-to-overcome-griefs-health-damaging-effects

About the Author

Cindi Dawson is an author, speaker, and teacher. She has been writing books since she was 15. Growing up in a Christian home with a bi-vocational industrial engineer / pastor father and a stay-at-home mother, she and her three sisters were introduced to the joys and sorrows of life early on by visiting hospitals, nursing homes, and homebound church members.

She grew up in Texas but spent most of her weekends in Oklahoma where her father pastored, providing the best of both worlds – the city and the country. The drive to Oklahoma provided time for her and her sisters to practice trios and quartets they would share that Sunday.

She felt led to write this book when she lost her mother, business partner, and father in nine months. After making a long list of what worked and what didn't work while experiencing Anticipatory Grief, she decided to share that list which became this book.

Currently she lives in the Shenandoah Valley between the Blue Ridge mountains of Virginia and the Alleghany mountains of West Virginia, where she hopes to spend the rest of her life. When not writing or speaking, she can be found singing, reading, and spending time laughing with friends.

Made in the USA
Columbia, SC
04 August 2024